China Academic Library

This book series collects, organizes and presents the master pieces in contemporary China studies. Titles in this series include those by Chinese authors who studied and worked abroad during early times whose works were originally in English and had already made great impacts in the Western world, such as Hu Shi, Fei Xiaotong and others; as well as works by more recent authors, Chinese and non-Chinese, that are of critical intellectual importance in introducing and understanding the transformation of the modern Chinese society. A wide variety of topics are covered by the series, from philosophy, economics, and history to law, cultural geography and regional politics. This series is a key English language resource for researchers and students in China studies and related subjects, as well as for general interest readers. The book series is a cooperation project between Springer and Foreign Language Teaching and Research Publishing Co., Ltd.

More information about this series at http://www.springer.com/series/11562

Yunxian Chen

New Economic Engine: Effective Government and Efficient Market

外语教学与研究出版社
FOREIGN LANGUAGE TEACHING AND RESEARCH PRESS

Springer

Yunxian Chen
School of Economics
Peking University
Beijing, China

ISSN 2195-1853 ISSN 2195-1861 (electronic)
China Academic Library
ISBN 978-981-15-2924-5 ISBN 978-981-15-2922-1 (eBook)
https://doi.org/10.1007/978-981-15-2922-1

Jointly published with Foreign Language Teaching and Research Publishing Co., Ltd.
The print edition is not for sale in China Mainland. Customers from China Mainland please order the print book from: Foreign Language Teaching and Research Publishing Co., Ltd.

This Springer imprint is published by the registered company Springer Nature Singapore Pte Ltd.
The registered company address is: 152 Beach Road, #21-01/04 Gateway East, Singapore 189721, Singapore

Preface

There are at least three main highlights in *New Economic Engine: Effective Government and Efficient Market*.

Breaking Through the Limitations of the Mainstream Western Economics System and the Market Theory Framework

The book is divided into nine chapters and one appendix. Chapter 1 looks at how Adam Smith's third book attempted to analyze the dealings of government and explores the roles governments should play and their functions. Chapter 2 reveals that John Maynard Keynes did not explain why national governments should participate or even be one of the main subjects in promoting infrastructure investment and construction, but he hastily launched a series of measures of governmental intervention in effective demand. Chapter 3 explicitly states that "resource generation" research is virgin ground in current mainstream economic theories. Chapter 4 points out that the government is a competitor in the field of "generative resources." Chapter 5 describes government competition in its broad and narrow senses. Chapter 6 describes the three levels of an efficient market. Chapter 7 describes the three levels of performance for an effective government. Chapter 8 expresses the view that there are nine modes of combinations of an effective government and an efficient market. Chapter 9 proposes the need to build up the new economic engine in the field of generative resources. The appendix proposes to build up the framework of "mezzoeconomics."

In its entirety, the book breaks through the limitations of the Western mainstream economics system and the market theory framework. Firstly, as to the theory of the market economy, this book suggests that a mature market economy is an "effective government plus efficient market" economy. Specifically, this book analyzes the "horizontal system of market economy," that is, resource allocation, resource scarcity, resource generation, and the roles of livelihood economy, industrial economy, urban economy, and others in the horizontal system of the market. It explores the "vertical system of market economy," that is, the market factor system, market organization system, market legal system, market supervision system, market environment system, and market infrastructure. These six subsystems form an organic whole in which market rules exert their effects and realize openness, fairness, and justice. It analyzes the "dual competitors in the market," that is, the main competitor in industrial economy is the enterprise, and the main competitor in urban economy is the government; the two competitors are distinguishable from each other, and yet interrelated, becoming the dual driving forces behind the industrial upgrading and national development across the world. It points out that both industrial and urban economic competitions must abide by the rules of the market; enterprises and governments, being the dual main competitors, must firstly abide by the rules of the market, participate in market competition, and at the same time, governments should function in a better way. It suggests that many theoretical and practical problems faced by nations in their economic development are not the problems of the market itself, but stem from defects of traditional market theory and a void of modern market theory.

Secondly, as to the economics system, the book proposes to establish a "mezzoeconomics" framework: Microeconomics takes the industrial economy as the carrier and develops a fairly complete discussion from the analysis of commodities, prices, supply and demand, competition, and equilibrium; while macroeconomics, under the circumstances of economic globalization, is feasible on one hand, but needs reform and innovation on the other hand. Henceforth, a mezzoeconomics system should be established, in which the effects of government competition are demonstrated in the allocation of newly generated resources, with regional economy or urban economy as its operating carrier, regional government as one of the main competitors. It has a positive effect of innovation and development on correcting the defects of the traditional economics system and filling the void left by the existing economics system.

Finally, as to economic growth across the world, this book puts forward the theory of a new economic engine. This new engine is in the field of resource generation, different from the industrial economy and livelihood economy. It is manifested at the current stage in the development of the urban economy, whose main content is the investment and construction of software and hardware infrastructure and the development and operation of intelligent cities (followed by the development and operation of space resources, deep-sea resources, polar economy, and network economy). This new engine is a new pole of economic growth for the world. Thus, every effort should be made to promote new engines on investments, innovations, and regulations with infrastructure development and construction as the main content. It is different from the "trade engine" and will promote sustainable economic growth across the world.

Correctly Explaining the Successful Experience of China's Reform and Opening Up Over the Past 40 Years from an Economic Perspective

This book explores the dual attributes of regional governments. Regional governments, in comparison with the world or the central government, are "quasi-macro" and "quasi-micro." The "quasi-macro" attribute emphasizes "coordination"; the "quasi-micro" attribute emphasizes "interests." Such dual attributes prompt regional governments to implement policies of "general underpinning, fairness and justice, and effective promotion" in the livelihood economy, "planning and guidance, support and coordination, supervision and management" in the industrial economy, and "participation in the competition, supervision in allocation" in the urban economy.

This book analyzes the dual competitions in the market. In the industrial economy, there is market competition with enterprises as main competitors, and in the urban economy, there is market competition with governments as main competitors. Through the buildup of the "new economic engine" mentioned above, governments continuously explore new economic growth points and promote the sustainable growth of the national economy.

This book points out that a mature market economy must be an organic integration of strong effective governments with strong efficient markets that operates in an orderly manner. In accordance with the major functions of the six subsystems of the modern market system, efficient market can be divided into three levels: "weak," "semi-strong," and "strong." In accordance with whether or not there are supporting policies and measures for livelihood economy, industrial economy, and urban economy, effective government can be divided into three levels: "weak," "semi-strong," and "strong." The organic combinations of the two form the nine modes of "effective government plus efficient market." Among these, "strong effective government plus strong efficient market" is the targeted mode for a mature market economy. It can be said that up until the present, China's market economic mode still needs to be upgraded, while the US market economic mode is not yet a mature market economy.

This book puts forward the view of government foresighted leading (GFL). The premise of government foresighted leading is to rely on market rules and market mechanism. The principles of government foresighted leading are that the market decides the allocation of resources, and at the same time, the government guides, adjusts, and forewarns in the industrial economy, allocates, participates in, and maintains order in the urban economy, and guarantees, underpins, and promotes in the livelihood economy. The measures of government foresighted leading are to use policies of planning, investment, consumption, price, taxation, interest rate, exchange rate, law, and others to innovate in value, institution, organization, and technology. The purpose of government foresighted leading is to promote the structural reform on the supply side or demand side, forming the leading edge in economic growth and a path toward scientific and sustainable development. This ensures that enterprises do what they should do, and governments do what enterprises cannot do and what enterprises cannot do well; neither of them can be absent.

This book explores innovation in government competition and points out that the government competes in nine aspects, including competitions in projects, supporting industrial chains, talent, science and technology, treasury and finance, infrastructure, imports and exports, environmental systems, policy systems, and management efficiencies. Governments in competition need to innovate constantly: "Innovations in values" substantially promote resource allocation during a nation's factor-driven stage, "innovations in organizational management" have multiplier effects on resource allocation during a nation's investment-driven stage, and "innovations in institutions and technologies" have crucial effects on resource allocation during a nation's innovation-driven stage. Continuous all-round innovations throughout the process in all factors can promote scientific and sustainable development of resource allocation at various stages of development across the world.

Developing a New Economics System and Market Theory with China Providing Extensive Materials for Its Development (Though Not Uniquely Chinese)

This book develops a mezzoeconomics system and modern market theory, which breaks away from the fields of Adam Smith's industrial economy or microeconomics, while completely differing from the theoretical nature, research focus, government behavior, and operation modes of the Keynesian government intervention theory. It can be said that this book is devoted to exploring the revolutionary innovation of market economy theory and economics system.

The American economist, Milton Friedman, commented that whoever accurately explained China's reform and development would win a Nobel Prize in Economics. China's economic development has become an important phenomenon in the world economy. The theoretical research and empirical analysis of China's economic development will certainly become one of the important achievements of world economic theories, which needs to be based on the exploration of China's reform and opening up, economic development and mode of operation, and also needs to learn from the practical development and research findings of the world economy. The great era has provided us with all of these.

Many people describe my life as "three-staged." Since the reform and opening up, I have spent more than 10 years in universities, more than 10 years in financial enterprises, and more than 10 years in the government; at the same time, I have studied at Harvard University, Yale University, the University of Massachusetts in the USA, and Toronto University in Canada successively. Henceforth, this humble book of not many words, not only discusses the economic situations in countries like the USA, Britain, Germany, ROK, Singapore, and organizations such as the World Bank and the International Monetary Fund; but also follows the course of my work, thought, research in practice, and distillation in analysis in the forefront of China's reform and opening up with my experience as Secretary of Shunde District Committee of the CPC, Secretary of Foshan Municipal Committee of the CPC and Mayor of Foshan City, and Vice-Governor of Guangdong Province.

The relationship between government and market is like Goldbach's conjecture in economics. From the definitions of the three types of resources in the world to the characteristics of resource allocation at various stages of economic development across the world, this book reveals the dual economic attributes of the government and points out that there are dual competitors in the market, and that, a mature market economy needs the organic combination of strong effective government and strong efficient market; that successful governments across the world cannot do without foresighted leading, and that governments need to compete in innovations and innovate in competitions. Thereby, new economic growth points and new paths to new economic engines can be found in the field of resource generation across the world. China's reform and opening up and innovative developments have provided a wide range of materials and resources for this theory; the results of this research will be integrated into world economic theories and serve the economic development and economic growth across the world.

Beijing, China — Yunxian Chen

Contents

1 What Could Be the Contents of Adam Smith's Third Book? 1
1 The Biography of Adam Smith ... 1
2 Analysis of the Contents of Adam Smith's Third Book ... 3
3 The Deficiencies in Adam Smith's Theories and Emergence of John Maynard Keynes' Theories ... 8

2 The Contributions and Deficiencies of Keynesian Economics 11
1 The Main Experiences of Keynes ... 11
2 Characteristics of Keynes' Economic Thoughts ... 12
3 Roosevelt's New Deal ... 14
4 Contributions and Deficiencies of Keynesian Economics ... 16

3 Scarcity and Generation of Resources ... 23
1 Scarcity and Generation of Resources Are a Pair of Twins in Resource Allocation ... 23
2 From Resource Generation to Generative Resources ... 25
3 Three Types of Resources in Cities ... 27
4 The Investment Entities of Urban Infrastructure ... 29

4 The Dual Attributes of Government ... 33
1 The Three Functions of Regional Governments ... 33
2 The Dual Roles of Regional Governments ... 36
3 The Dual Competitors in Market Competition ... 39
4 Thoughts from Three Case Studies ... 42

5 Regional Government Competition ... 45
1 The Broad and Narrow Senses of Government Competition ... 45
2 The Connections and Differences Between Government Competition and Enterprise Competition ... 48
3 The Forms of Regional Government Competition ... 50
4 "Voting by Foot" to Select Regional Governments ... 54

6 Modern Market Economy 57
1 The Horizontal System of Modern Market 57
2 The Vertical System of Modern Market 59
3 Efficient Market Division 62
4 Re-understanding Market Failure 64

7 Mature Effective Governments 69
1 The Types of Effective Governments 69
2 Government Foresighted Leading (GFL) 71
3 Innovation is Competitiveness 77
4 Government Failure Revisited 79

8 The Choices of Effective Government and Efficient Market Modes 83
1 Potential Economic Growth Rate and Real Economic Growth Rate 83
2 Washington Consensus and the Middle Income Trap 84
3 The Combination and Assessment of "Effective Government Plus Efficient Market" Mode 88
4 Strong Effective Government Plus Strong Efficient Market Equals Mature Market Economy 90

9 Building Up a New Engine for Global Economic Development 95
1 Kindleberger Trap and Endogenous Growth Theory 95
2 The Arrival of the Era of Urbanization-Led Economic Growth 98
3 Community of National Interests 99
4 Building Up a New Engine for Global Economic Development 102

Appendix On Microeconomics, Mezzoeconomics, and Macroeconomics 109

Epilogue 119

Chapter 1
What Could Be the Contents of Adam Smith's Third Book?

1 The Biography of Adam Smith

Adam Smith (1723–1790), renowned English social philosopher and political economist, is the key representative figure of classical political economics.

Adam Smith's father was a customs controller in Scotland, and his mother was the daughter of a hereditary landowner. At the age of 14, Adam Smith became a student at the University of Glasgow, receiving a good education in this famous center of Enlightenment. There, Smith was moved by his mentor, Francis Hutcheson, a renowned moral philosopher, whose philosophy profoundly influenced his subsequent moral philosophy and economic views.

In 1740, Adam Smith graduated from the University of Glasgow with honors and went to Oxford to continue his education. There, he relentlessly self-educated and explored, acquiring substantial amounts of knowledge in classical and contemporary philosophy.

In 1751, aged 28, Adam Smith was appointed professor of logic at the University of Glasgow. In 1752, he turned to the field of moral philosophy to research in natural theology, ethics, jurisprudence and political economics.

In 1759, aged 36, Smith published his first work, *The Theory of Moral Sentiments*. This work laid the foundation in psychological behavior analysis for his later book, *The Wealth of Nations*.

In 1776, aged 53, Smith completed the famous *An Inquiry into the Nature and Causes of the Wealth of Nations*, which continually exerts important influence even to this day. This book looked deeply into the behavior of market economy and the complex political economics system, rendering Adam Smith a towering figure in the history of economic thoughts even to this day.

Upon completing his second masterpiece, Smith spent more than ten years exploring, thinking and investigating, and attempted to write a third book speculated to be on "the general principles of law and government". In 1790, at the age of 67 however, Smith's life, filled with honors and recognition, ended with a little pity.

Y. Chen, *New Economic Engine: Effective Government and Efficient Market*, China Academic Library, https://doi.org/10.1007/978-981-15-2922-1_1

In accordance with the custom at that place of his time, Smith's files and his personal possessions were destroyed rather than preserved following his passing. This rendered his unfinished third book and its core ideas a conjecture for later generations.

Adam Smith's biography described him as a man who was totally oblivious and paid little attention to all things other than those associated with learning and acquiring knowledge. He would be in a ball and might not even recognize his dance partner; he might unwittingly add butter and bread into the teapot when making tea, and complain later about the poor taste; he might be taking a morning stroll and whilst enjoying a deep breath of fresh air, fall into a bout of deep contemplation only to realize he had already ventured 15 miles away from home still dressed in his night gown. During his tenure as Commissioner of Customs, he received numerous gun salutes, and possibly in his attempt to reciprocate the gesture, performed an elaborate drill with his cane. Delivering papers and speeches in unfamiliar surrounds, Smith would initially stutter out of shyness, but once he familiarized himself with the surrounds, he would speak eloquently, fluently and uninhibitedly.[1]

During Adam Smith's era in the 18th century, Britain was experiencing a transition from workshop handicraft to mechanical industry. In the early 18th century, France and Germany remained at an infantile feudal stage dominated by cottage handicraft. Britain, on the other hand, had entered capitalist stage where workshop handicraft had developed in cities across the nation. Under the direction of a capitalist, many workers used simple tools to cooperate with due division of labor in a workshop. This is the characteristic of workshop handicraft. Such a scenario continued until 1760, when the Industrial Revolution took place and industries using machineries emerged. At that time, Britain was not only the center of world trade, but a leading industrialized country.

What can be concluded is that: (1) Adam Smith lived during the era of the onset of the British Industrial Revolution. Industrialization just commenced, though urbanization did not. It was precisely the moment at the onset of revolution. (2) Adam Smith's father was a customs controller, and his mother was the daughter of a rich landowner from a family with substantial wealth and social status. As the revolution started and unfolded, Adam Smith did not show any obvious inclination towards the pursuit of wealth, but was instead immersed in academia and learning. (3) Adam Smith produced only three books in his lifetime, each of which took him more than 10 years of intense research. He was already a university professor at the age of 28, and completed his first book *The Theory of Moral Sentiments* at the age of 36, investigating the social behavior and moral sentiments of people. Subsequently, Adam Smith turned his attention towards commodity pricing, supply and demand, competition, market, and the behaviors of industries, and ventured into the circle of businessmen in London; 17 years later, aged 53, he completed his second book *An Inquiry into the Nature and Causes of the Wealth of Nations*. Thereafter, not content with just enjoying the fame and fortune bestowed upon him by *The Wealth of Nations*, Adam Smith went to the customs, acknowledged then as the true source of wealth, where the import and export among nations were highly collectively reflected, and worked as a customs officer, just as his father did. There was speculation that, Adam

Smith worked as a customs officer for about 14 years, during which he studied government's duties, functions, powers, laws and regulations in practice, and at the age of 67, began writing his third book, *The General Principles of Law and Government*. Regrettably, the third book was never published. But what could be postulated was that, Smith has led a life of learning and contemplating, analyzing and revealing the attributes of the behavior of individuals, industries, and states, and the principles and laws governing the market and economic bodies.

2 Analysis of the Contents of Adam Smith's Third Book

Adam Smith's academic thoughts were influenced not only by the growing and booming British industry, the theories of the physiocratic school, especially François Quesnay's and Anne Robert Jacques Turgot's, and David Hume's trade and monetary theories; but in particular, the philosophy of his mentor at the University of Glasgow, Francis Hutcheson. The philosophy proposed by Francis Hutcheson that people themselves could discover what is ethically good by discovering the actions that serve the good of humankind, had profoundly shaped Adam Smith's research on (benevolent) behavior of individuals in society, (beneficial) behavior of industries in the market, and even his later attempt to analyze the (benevolent) behavior of government.

Adam Smith's First Book, *The Theory of Moral Sentiments*

The Theory of Moral Sentiments is made up of seven parts. The first part looks at the propriety of actions. The second part discusses merits and demerits, that is, the objects of rewards and punishment. The third part talks about the foundation of our judgments concerning our own sentiments and conduct, and the sense of duty. The fourth part relates the effects of utility on the sentiment of approbation. The fifth part goes into the influence of custom and fashion on the sentiments of moral approbation and disapprobation. The sixth part defines character of virtue. The seventh part investigates systems of moral philosophy.

In the book, Adam Smith uses human emotions and empathies as the basic principle to decipher the roots of justice, benevolence, self-denial, and other moral sentiments, explain the nature and principles of moral evaluation and the characteristics of virtues, and introduce and evaluate other schools of thoughts on moral philosophy, revealing the foundation on which human society maintains and develops harmoniously, and some basic morals humans should adhere to.

Concepts such as "human nature", "one's own behavior", "self-preservation", "selfishness", "inner self", "impartial spectator", "self-control", "sympathy", "inner conflict", "profit seeker", "invisible hand" "empathy", "social creatures", etc., are key words in the book. Compassion, being an invisible hand, is regulating individual social behavior, promoting the organic integration of selfishness and sympathy, thereby defining the essence of human nature. Through this book, Adam Smith, for the first time, presents and demonstrates the philosophy imparted by his mentor,

Francis Hutcheson, that people themselves could discover what is ethically good by discovering the actions that serve the good of humankind.

Adam Smith's Second Book, *An Inquiry into the Nature and Causes of the Wealth of Nations*

The Wealth of Nations is divided into five parts. Book I (11 chapters in total) describes the causes of improvement in the productive powers of labor, and of the order by which its produce is naturally distributed among the different ranks of the people; Book II (5 chapters in total) examines the nature, accumulation and employment of stock; Book III (4 chapters in total) distinguishes different progress of opulence in different nations; Book IV (9 chapters in total) elaborates on systems of political economy; Book V (3 chapters in total) discusses the revenue of the sovereign or commonwealth, which is closely related to our subject here. In Book V, Chapter 1 is on the expenses of the sovereign or commonwealth. Specifically, Part 1 is on the expense of defense, Part 2 on the expense of justice, Part 3 on the expenses of public works and public institutions with Article 1 on the expenses of public works and institutions for facilitating the commerce of the society, Article 2 on the expense of the institutions for the education of youth, Article 3 on the expense of the institutions for the instruction of people of all ages, and Part 4 on the expense of supporting the dignity of the sovereign. Chapter 2 then probes into the sources of the general or public revenue of the society; and Chap. 3 examines public debts.

The main economic ideas conveyed in *The Wealth of Nations* are: (1) Division of Labor and Value Theory. It includes Division of Labor Theory, Value Theory (value in use and value in exchange; value of labor and the setting of two types of values), Theory on the Three Sources of Revenue (namely wages, profit and rent), and Market Price and Natural Price. (2) Income and Allocation Theory. This includes Wages Theory, Profit Theory, and Rent Theory. (3) Regeneration of Social Capital Theory. This comprises "What is regeneration of social capital", "Premise on the theory of Regeneration of Social Capital", and "The core problem in the regeneration of social capital is the problem in realizing the aggregate social product", etc.

The main ideas presented in *The Wealth of Nations* are that a seemingly chaotic free market is in fact a self-adjusting mechanism producing types and quantities of products determined by what society needs most urgently, leading everyone through pricing, demand and supply, and competition just like an invisible hand, to follow market rules conscientiously. In Adam Smith's own words, "As every individual, therefore, endeavors as much as he can both to employ his capital in the support of domestic industry, and so to direct that industry that its produce may be of the greatest value; every individual necessarily labours to render the annual revenue of the society as great as he can. …and he is in this, as in many other cases, led by an invisible hand to promote an end which was no part of his intention. … By pursuing his own interest, he frequently promotes that of the society more effectually than when he really intends to promote it."[2] As seen here, the mechanism of price, demand and supply, and competition, being the invisible hand, is governing the behavior of commodity producers/enterprises, leading to an organic integration of egoism and altruism, henceforth, forming the basic connotation of the free economy. Adam Smith has taken the concept of "an invisible hand" from *The Moral Sentiments* and aptly applied to *The Wealth of Nations*, in the self-adjustment and self-regulation of market economy, demonstrating once again his mentor Francis Hutcheson's philosophy that people themselves could discover what is ethically good by discovering the actions that serve the good of humankind.

Under the premise of economic liberalism mentioned in *The Wealth of Nations*, Adam Smith points out the government functions in a free economy society, covered mainly in Chapter 1 of Book V. This chapter deals with expenses of defense, justice, and public works and public institutions (expenses of education included), etc. It also summarizes the three main functions of the government, that is, ensuring national security, maintaining justice and order, and providing public goods. Amongst these, the profit of erecting and maintaining public works such as roads, bridges, navigable canals, and harbors could never repay the expense to any individual, therefore the duty should be taken by the state.[3] Henceforth, the government plays the role of a night watchman. This particular role of the government is mentioned in Book V of *The Wealth of Nations*, generalized by later generations as "small government".

The book established Adam Smith as the forefather of classical economics, and the founder of classical economics and market value theory. On this basis, later generations have made up for Adam Smith's deficiencies such as the inadequacies of the division of labor theory, the inherent contradictions in the value theory system and the weaknesses in the market economy theory, leading to the mainstream neoclassical economics of today; and his overview of the functions and roles of the government in the market economy still exerts its influence some 240 years later. Traditional economists still adopt "small government", "night watchman state", and "provision of public goods" to keep tabs on the roles of modern countries in the market economy.

Adam Smith's Third Book, *Analysis of the Contents*

Adam Smith completed his first book, *The Theory of Moral Sentiments* in 1759 and his second book, *The Wealth of Nations* in 1776. Thereafter, he returned from London to Scotland, and worked at the customs where his father had worked previously, a place considered then to be the true source of wealth, and an important import and export trading place where national interests are highly concentrated. There, he observed and contemplated, hoping to write a third book on the subject of "the general principles of law and government, and of the different revolutions they have undergone in the different ages and periods of society."[4] Regrettably, he had passed away before his third book was completed, and furthermore, his manuscripts were all destroyed.

What could be the contents of Adam Smith's third book? References need to be made once again to the philosophy instructed by his mentor, Francis Hutcheson, that people themselves could discover what is ethically good by discovering the actions that serve the good of humankind. Henceforth, in *The Moral Sentiments*, through analyzing a person's selfishness and sympathy for others in society, Adam Smith formulated the basic connotation of human nature theory and the characteristics of morality; in *The Wealth of Nations*, through investigating industries' egoism and altruism in the market, Smith formulated the basic connotation of the free economy and the characteristics of industries' commercial behaviors; then, through analyzing national and human interests, would his third book on "government and law" be on the basic national economic functions and the characteristics of management practice of government (law)? At the center of Adam Smith's political economics is the concept of the "invisible hand": as to human's moral behaviors, Adam Smith suggested that the "invisible hand" integrates selfishness and sympathy, which is guiding human moral sentiments; as to industries' commercial behaviors, Adam Smith suggested that the "invisible hand" integrates egoism and altruism, which is the guiding mechanism on pricing, demand and supply, and competition for industries. In that case, as to government management practice, what would the "invisible hand" be? Analyzing Adam Smith's own academic thoughts and the philosophy imparted by his mentor in conjunction, it appears that Adam Smith was investigating "behavioral science"; or was perhaps revealing human nature, industries in the market, and state management by investigating "behavioral science" and "behavioral economics". Regrettably, he only left footprints on two of his three giant steps in his two masterpieces.

We can at least conclude that had Adam Smith completed his third masterpiece, his analysis on government functions and management would not be merely confined to what was described in the first chapter of Book V of *The Wealth of Nations*. Apart from national protection and maintaining justice and order, government's provision of public goods would definitely not be confined to just the four types of infrastructure—roads, bridges, navigable canals and harbors, which yield no profit to capitalists. What is regrettable is that even today, over 200 years later, various economic thoughts on government functions and management practice have not gone beyond what Adam Smith had described in *The Wealth of Nations*.

The limitations of research on government functions and its characteristics of behaviors when Adam Smith wrote *The Wealth of Nations* was understandable. Firstly, the Industrial Revolution had just started, small handicraft workshops were just shifting to large-scale industries using machineries, urbanization was still in its infancy, and people still focused on industries, industrial resources, and industrial revolution. Just as Adam Smith had criticized mercantilism, which viewed trade as the only source of wealth, and physiocracy, which viewed agriculture as the only wealth-creator by pointing out that all the material production departments create wealth, *The Wealth of Nations* lacked the recognition and application of urban infrastructure and urban resources. Because of limitations of the times, Adam Smith restricted government functions and management practice only to industrial economy. Secondly, faced with industrial economy, namely, industries, commodities, pricing, demand and supply, and competition, governments would naturally restrict their roles as night watchmen in ensuring national security, justice, and order, and in providing a conducive market, and nothing else.

The problem now is precisely that after the completion of *The Wealth of Nations* in 1776, Adam Smith shifted his attention from the study of human behavior to the study of industry behavior, then to the study of government behavior, and began writing on "general principles of government and law" in 1790, more than ten years after the completion of *The Wealth of Nations*. Why did Adam Smith work for the customs after he completed *The Wealth of Nations*? Was it just to take care of his mother? Was it to make more money? From the trajectory of his life, these were obviously not the main reasons. When Adam Smith completed *The Moral Sentiments* at the age of 36, he became a private teacher to the son of the Chancellor of the Exchequer, and gained a salary for life. To research for *The Wealth of Nations*, he socialized with London's business circle, and completed the masterpiece when he was 53. Thereafter, he chose to work for the customs, where a country's import and export could be observed, and presumably began to research on domestic and international economic situations, and the "government behavior" derived from them. This manifested that his life choices were mainly correlated with his academic interest. Why did it take him 14 years to research for his third book? Of course, during his research, Adam Smith was also responsible for some school matters. More importantly, however, in my opinion, he tried to apply further the philosophy of his mentor, Francis Hutcheson, that people themselves could discover what is ethically good by discovering the actions that serve the good of humankind to the rules of government management and operation.

If the essence of *The Moral Sentiments* was the guidance of "an invisible hand", which is the amalgamation of individuals and society, selfishness and sympathy; and the essence of *The Wealth of Nations* was the promotion of "an invisible hand", which is the amalgamation of industries and market, egoism and altruism; then, what was the driving force behind a government's behavior attributes and nature? What was regulating the internal restraints between countries? For a government, there are national interests as well as international interests; it has national attributes as well as international attributes; it embodies partial (micro) demand while expecting overall (macro) balance. The essence is the contradiction of national interests of one country against another, and even against human interests. Furthermore, when a state pursues and protects its own interests, apart from political and military means, what kind of economic means are there at its disposal? How does a state pursue its own interests? Possible routes include "protection" and "competition". While "protecting" its own interests should be promoted by mutual rules, how should it "compete" for its own interests? In what areas should it compete? I think these were the difficult questions encountered by Adam Smith in his third book, which he endeavored to solve. However, he couldn't or had no time to answer these questions. As a consequence, there exist the fallacy of traditional economics and the shortcomings in Adam Smith's market theory. That is, there is only one subject—"industry" with industry supply and demand, and industry competition in the market. This fallacy in market theory lasts even to this day. Many problems in modern economy are not problems of the market, but fallacies in traditional market theory, problems that the much revered and esteemed Adam Smith left behind.

3 The Deficiencies in Adam Smith's Theories and Emergence of John Maynard Keynes' Theories

Adam Smith is the forefather of classical economics and the founder of market value theory. The core of his theory and even its deficiencies have influenced generations that came and went. Many economists that followed, including the renowned Professor Alfred Marshall who published *Principles of Economics* in 1890, made "Economics" an independent discipline, proposed a series of new categories and concepts, boldly innovated and promoted the study of economics to a new level, and in doing so, formed the school of Neoclassical Economics. However, in my opinion, these were just reforms and innovations, and synthesized theories under the original framework established by Adam Smith. The new school merely studied commodities, pricing, demand and supply, competition in terms of industries, industrial economy and industrial resources; it was restrained to the relationships between the markets (industries) and governments—the "Goldbach's conjecture" in economics, though the discussions were deepened or extended by changing perspectives or innovating categories. Thus the government was limited and only deemed as the "night watchman" or "small government" who provided security, fairness, order and public goods.

The biggest contribution made by Adam Smith's *Wealth of Nations* was its elaborate description of market attributes, industries and their relationships with the government in the industrial economy. Under the guidance of "an invisible hand", the market attributes and government functions in the industrial economy were clearly defined. This is the reason why Adam Smith's economic thoughts are everlasting! However, it could not distinguish other forms of economies from industrial economy or had not done so; it had not detailed the complete connotation of the market system, the boundaries (or scope) of the market, and the effectiveness of the market, nor had it intricately defined the clear relationships between governments and the market, etc. The constraints of the times and the uncompleted third book lay behind the big flaw in Adam Smith's economic theory.

John Maynard Keynes, with his unique experiences in academia and politics, completed *The Economic Consequences of the Peace* in 1919 after World War I; to deal with the world economic crisis of 1929–1933 and promote Roosevelt's "New Deal" in the United States, he completed *The General Theory of Employment, Interest and Money* in 1936. The deficiencies in Adam Smith's economic theory, or what had remained unexplored, led to Keynes' success; whilst Keynes' theory had made breakthroughs in economics, it was also stuck in its deficiencies and contradictions.

Notes

1. Ian Simpson Ross. *The Life of Adam Smith.* New York: Oxford University Press Inc., 2010, pp. 240, 254, 333.
2. Adam Smith. *An Inquiry into the Nature and Causes of the Wealth of Nations.* Chicago: University of Chicago Press, 1977, pp. 590, 593–594.

3. Ibid. pp. 963–964.
4. Robert L. Heilbroner. "Adam Smith", Encyclopedia Britannica, Jun. 13, 2019, https://www.britannica.com/biography/Adam-Smith.

Chapter 2
The Contributions and Deficiencies of Keynesian Economics

1 The Main Experiences of Keynes

John Maynard Keynes (1883–1946), born and raised in Cambridge, England, was highly proficient and competent in mathematics and economics. From 1902 to 1906, aged 19 to 23, Keynes studied at Cambridge University; after graduation, from 1906 to 1908, Keynes worked as a clerk in the India Office. Keynes returned to work in Cambridge University in 1908. In 1913, aged 30, Keynes published his first work, *Indian Currency and Finance*. From 1913 to 1914, he worked for the Royal Commission on Indian Currency and Finance.

From 1915 onward, that is, during the First World War, Keynes worked for the Treasury and later took charge of foreign financial relations. In May of 1919, aged 36, as the chief representative of the British Treasury as well as an advisor to Prime Minister David Lloyd George, Keynes attended the Paris Peace Conference, during which he attempted to reduce the huge amount of compensation Entente Powers had demanded from Germany. The claim was refused and Keynes resigned. In 1919, Keynes returned to Cambridge University and published the book, *The Economic Consequences of the Peace*; thereafter, he published a series of articles and works such as *A Treatise on Probability* in 1921, *A Revision of the Treaty* in 1922, *A Tract on Monetary Reform* in 1923, "Does Unemployment Need a Drastic Remedy?" in 1924, and *The End of Laissez-Faire* in 1926, and *A Treatise on Money* in 1930, etc.

In October of 1929, the Wall Street Stock Market crashed, and a world economic depression started. In 1930, Keynes became a member of the Economic Advisory Council. In 1931, at the invitation of the University of Chicago, Keynes travelled to Chicago to discuss crisis-combating measures with American economists. From 1932 to 1933, Keynes advocated continually government's intervention in stimulating economic growth; in 1934, Keynes visited President Roosevelt to promote the New Deal on his second trip to the United States. In February of 1936, *The General Theory of Employment, Interest and Money* was published.

Y. Chen, *New Economic Engine: Effective Government and Efficient Market*, China Academic Library, https://doi.org/10.1007/978-981-15-2922-1_2

In September of 1939, the Second World War started; in 1940, Keynes was given a position at the Treasury again and became a consultant of the Chancellor. From 1942 to 1944, Keynes actively engaged in building post-war economic order, from which the later International Monetary Fund (IMF), the World Bank and the Bretton Woods system were derived. In February of 1946, Keynes went to the United States to attend the first meeting of the World Bank and International Monetary Fund. In April of 1946, John Maynard Keynes passed away.

2 Characteristics of Keynes' Economic Thoughts

Keynes' strengths in mathematics and economics, coupled with his rich experiences in academia and politics, led him to contemplate and explore economics in a unique way. For example:

(1) Earlier in his book, *The Economic Consequences of the Peace* in 1919, Keynes had already made a detailed analysis of pre-war Europe, the Paris Peace Conference, the items of the Treaty of Versailles, especially those on war reparations, and the prospect of Europe after signing the Treaty and remedies, etc. He believed that the huge claims Entente Powers demanded would destroy Germany's economy, thereby leading to further conflicts in Europe. He proposed to revise relevant items of the Treaty, resolve debts between countries, make international loans available, and improve relations with Russia to remedy hidden troubles brought about by the Treaty.[1] Through *The Economic Consequences of the Peace*, we can see that: (i) Keynes predicted profoundly the serious consequences that might be brought about by government actions that did not conform to economic logic. Hence, he was trying to prevent and remedy such situations. (ii) Keynes analyzed government actions and attempted to change the possible consequences with government's economic policies and measures. In doing so, he raised to a higher level the general public's (especially of that time) awareness and acceptance of economics. (iii) Keynes described the roles and functions of the government from the perspectives of state power and overall economic trends, thereby breaking away from the traditional economic theory and objectively analyzing how government's policies directly affected national economy.

(2) Faced with the situation of a million unemployed Britons in 1924, Keynes, in his article, "Does Unemployment Need a Drastic Remedy?", proposed the government should spend 100 million pounds per year to stimulate economic growth, especially in investing in and building housing, roads, and electric energy facilities, etc. Keynes further suggested that national savings should be spent on domestic infrastructure instead of foreign investment. Governments should do what the private investors could not do or have not done yet, and increasingly raise their effectiveness.[2] Here, (i) Keynes further suggested that government's

measures to stimulate economic growth could be to increase domestic investments in constructing infrastructure such as housing, roads, and electric energy facilities. (ii) The operation organizations of public infrastructure are semi-autonomous entities, invested by private funds and administered by the government. The investment and construction of public goods could effectively stimulate economic growth. (iii) Thus, governments should not do things which private investors have already done. It doesn't matter whether they do better or worse than the private investors. But instead, they should do the things that modern society needs to do but has not yet started doing. Henceforth, Keynes has achieved a breakthrough in the field of economics by looking into the effects of government's investment in infrastructure construction on stimulating economic growth, and attempting to explain these under a theoretical framework.

(3) Keynes published *The General Theory of Employment, Interest and Money* in 1936, which is divided into 6 Books made up of 24 chapters. Book I is Introduction, explaining mainly the effective demand principle; Book II is Definitions and Ideas, elaborating mainly on the definitions of income, saving and investment, and the meaning of further investigation; Book III talks about the Propensity to Consume, elaborating mainly on marginal propensity to consume and the multiplier; Book IV investigates the Inducement to Invest, elaborating mainly on marginal efficiency of capital, liquidity preference, etc.; Book V is on Money-wages and Prices, elaborating mainly on money-wages, pricing and the employment function; Book VI is Short Notes Suggested by the General Theory, elaborating mainly on trade cycle, mercantilism, and the social philosophy towards which the general theory might lead. Some key issues worthy of note are: (i) Keynes, being a student of Professor Marshall in Cambridge, at this point held the view that the classical and neoclassical economic theories represented by Adam Smith and Alfred Marshall respectively, which state that an equilibrium state of full employment can be reached through self-adjustment mechanism of market demand and supply forces, cannot hold true. (ii) The level of employment in a country is determined by effective demand. Effective demand refers to the aggregate demand when aggregate supply price and aggregate demand price are in equilibrium. As aggregate supply will not change significantly in the short run, the root cause of underemployment lies in insufficient effective demand. (iii) Effective demand or aggregate demand is the sum of consumption demand and investment demand. Insufficient effective demand or aggregate demand is thus due to insufficient consumption demand and investment demand. (iv) Hence, Keynes advocated government's intervention in the economy. Through policies, the government can stimulate consumption and increase investment in order to attain full employment. Keynes believed that as consumption tendency is relatively stable in the short run, to attain full employment, the government must focus on increasing investment demand. Changes in investment will produce a multiplier effect on changes in income and output, with national income increasing a few times. (v) Keynes suggested that the government should increase investment with fiscal policies rather than monetary

policies. Especially during periods of economic depression, the government should adopt expansionary fiscal policies, that is to increase fiscal expenditure, reduce taxes and issue bonds. Keynes also suggested that investment policies should work in concert with consumption demand. Keynes felt that the government should also control investment, in order to prevent fluctuations of the economy brought about by it. (vi) The government must think of ways to increase effective demand, and increase consumption demand by improving equal income.

As can be seen, (i) in his *General Theory of Employment, Interest and Money*, Keynes found a new field to help promote economic growth for a country—this field is not in foreign trade advocated by mercantilism, nor in agricultural production favored by physiocrats, nor in industrial economy as Adam Smith described, but in public projects and goods that governments provide to the society that bring no profits to private investors, namely, investment in the construction of roads, bridges, navigable canals, habors, housing, power energy and other infrastructure as Adam Smith described in Article 1, Part 3, Chapter 1, Book V of *The Wealth of Nations*. (ii) The government should intervene in the development of the national economy, especially in situations of imbalanced aggregate demand and insufficient effective demand. The government should intervene in investments in infrastructure. (iii) And the government should adopt proactive fiscal policies like increasing fiscal expenditures, reducing taxes and issuing government bonds, to increase fiscal budgets for construction of housing, roads and other public projects. (iv) Keynes' characteristic economic thoughts, being an independent economic theory system, took shape. Keynes' theory, together with classical economics dominated by Adam Smith and neoclassical economics dominated by Alfred Marshall, formed the two sides of the economic system. One side focused on supplying commodities, forming industrial economics with enterprises being the subjects, each abiding by the rules of market economy. The other side focused on supplying public works and public goods, forming infrastructure economics or urban economics. Keynes did not make clear who the subjects were in infrastructure economics or urban economics: it could be the government, private investors or economic associations. Keynes again did not make clear the rules by which they abided, or maybe they also abided by the rules of market economy.

3 Roosevelt's New Deal

As described earlier, Keynes visited the United States on numerous occasions. In 1934, Keynes met President Roosevelt, and discussed and promoted his New Deal. On the one hand, President Roosevelt was very appreciative of Keynes' views; but on the other, Keynes was under hostility from American advocates of laissez-faire economy.

At the heart of Roosevelt's New Deal were the three Rs, a series of economic policies implemented by Franklin Roosevelt after he was elected President in 1933: "Recovery", "Relief", and "Reform", otherwise known as the "Three Rs New Deal". It would be most opportune to mention here that the failure of Hoover's government in combating the economic crisis was due to the government's pursuance of a laissez-faire policy, and its objection to intervening in the national economy, which in turn aggravated the damage done by the economic crisis and plunged the American economy to rock bottom. Increasing public displeasure and dissatisfaction led to public outcries for reform growing louder by the day; with the election slogan of the "New Deal", Roosevelt won widespread support and defeated Herbert C. Hoover to become the 32nd President of the United States.

Apart from revamping the banking and financial industries, revitalizing manufacturing industries and modifying agricultural policies, establishing a social security system and building emergency relief agencies, the most important measure in Roosevelt's New Deal was to promote "Work Relief", that is to put in massive efforts to build public works and increase employment in order to stimulate production and consumption.

Work Relief was a measure to revamp the previous federal scheme which merely transferred relief in cash and in kind across all states purely as a relief effort, to one that provided employment in public works construction to the unemployed, especially to fit and healthy young people aged from 18 to 25, with high unemployment rate. Such public works projects included flood control, soil and water conservation, road construction, and various types of work in forestation (tree planting, forest protection, fire break and forest watchtowers setup), as well as various public and civil works. This measure not only revamped the provision of relief across the country and encouraged the unemployed to develop the sense of self-reliance and independence, but also spurred the construction and development of public and civil works in the United States, and stimulated production and consumption, alleviating the economic crisis and social conflicts brought about by the Great Depression.

The first measure of Roosevelt's New Deal was to urge the Congress to pass the plan of "Civilian Conservation Corps". The plan recruited a first batch of 250 thousand people to work in 1500 camps across the various states in the country. Before the United States was involved in the Second World War, more than two million youths had worked in this project, opening up more than 7.4 million acres of state-owned forests and a large number of state-owned parks. Each person worked for an average of 9 months each session; most of their salaries was spent on supporting themselves and their families, thus expanding the scope of relief and correspondingly increasing the purchasing power across the whole society.

During the era of the New Deal, there were various institutions of work relief across the United States, generally divided into two systems: (1) the Public Works Department (with a budget of USD 4 billion allocated by the government), which was responsible for planning long-term objectives for public works, and (2) the Civil Engineering Department (with a budget of USD 1 billion allocated by the government), running 180,000 small-scale projects across the nation, including school buildings, bridges, dikes, sewerage systems, post offices and administration agencies. Employment for 4 million people was provided and a vast number of unemployed unskilled workers went back to work. Several new work relief programs were established subsequently. The most famous were the Works Progress Administration, which received a Congressional grant of USD 5 billion and the National Youth Administration, which targeted the youth of the nation. Both programs collectively employed a total of 23 million people, providing employment for half of the nation's workforce.

By the onset of World War II, the Federal Government had already provided USD 18 billion for various projects and comparatively inexpensive direct relief efforts. The United States government already built nearly 1,000 airports, more than 12,000 sports fields, and more than 800 school buildings and hospitals, not only creating employment for craftsmen, unskilled laborers and architects, but also providing a variety of jobs for thousands of unemployed artists. That was by far the grandest and most successful relief program the United States government has ever implemented. These funds, through various channels, stimulated private consumption and investment through government's investment.

The measures of Roosevelt's New Deal, especially a large number of public and civilian relief projects, such as the Tennessee Valley Comprehensive Development Project, not only greatly alleviated unemployment and stimulated economic recovery, but more importantly, created a new model for the government to intervene in the economy or stimulate economic growth. The use of active fiscal policies, combined with massive public works construction and provision of public goods, provided the theoretical basis and implementation means for the government's intervention in the economy or exploration for a new model of economic growth. Investments, especially infrastructure investments in public works and public facilities brought great benefits to the American economy, establishing Roosevelt as the most popular American president after Abraham Lincoln.

4 Contributions and Deficiencies of Keynesian Economics

There have been widespread media reports in recent years that Donald Trump's economics resembles Roosevelt's New Deal. According to "The Essence of Trump's Administration is Roosevelt rather than Reagan", an economic review published on March 7, 2017 in *The Weekly-Economist* of Japan, although Trump's Administration is often considered similar to Reagan's, Trump's policies are in fact more akin to Roosevelt's New Deal. "During the election campaign, both Reagan and Trump used the slogan, 'Make America Great Again' and ultimately achieved overwhelming victories. Furthermore, Reagan also talked about tax reductions and deregulations. In terms of patriotic slogans and some economic policies, Trump's Administration and that of Reagan do have their similarities. However, … the economic policies implemented by the Reagan's Administration, apart from tax reductions and deregulations, also included interest rates hikes, revaluation of the Dollar and fiscal tightening. … Reagan's economic policies focused on supply side rather than demand side, allowed industries to participate fully in market competition through thorough deregulation. ... If compared to the past, Trump's polices are similar to Democrat Roosevelt's New Deal following the 1929 global panic. The objective of the New Deal was to eliminate the extreme shortage in demand and unemployment, it was an economic policy centered on huge public expenditures and based on Keynesian demand side ideas. ... During the election campaign, Trump publicly committed USD 1 trillion to infrastructure investment, with the aim of strongly stimulating demand side. Although the United States has now recovered from the Lehman crisis, and almost approached full employment, nevertheless, there are still problems of mismatches in employment. Trump's policies can be said to be a 'New Deal', judging from the emphasis on demand side and deliberate attempts to employ workers. ... As to the movement of US interest rates, there could be a similar trend to the era of Roosevelt. ... Hence, in order to maximize the effectiveness of the policies, Trump is attempting to intervene in exchange rate movements (at least verbally), correcting excessive appreciation in the US dollar and high interest rates."[3]

Indeed, from the Roosevelt Administration to the Trump Administration, the economic rationale behind those measures to stimulate economic growth with massive amounts of infrastructure investments originated from the series of Keynesian theories, especially "Does Unemployment Need a Drastic Remedy?" of 1924 and *The General Theory of Employment, Interest and Money* published in 1936. Keynes' unique life experiences in academia and politics, and his pioneering "government intervention" economic thoughts, have made a great contribution to world economic theory and economic system.

Take *The General Theory of Employment, Interest and Money* as an example. It is generally believed that if Adam Smith's *Wealth of Nations* is the Bible of economic liberalism, then Keynes' *General Theory of Employment, Interest and Money* is the treasure of state interventionism. (1) Keynes reinterpreted the concept of full employment, and pointed out the three types of unemployment that existed in reality, namely, voluntary unemployment, frictional unemployment, and involuntary unemployment. The existence of involuntary unemployment meant that the traditional employment theory is invalid. (2) Keynes brought up the principle of effective demand, and pointed out that the level of employment depends on the effective demand of society, which is in equilibrium with aggregate supply. (3) Keynes suggested a simple national income determination theory, and stated that the main factors deciding national income and employment rate are three psychological laws (marginal propensity to consume, marginal efficiency of capital and liquidity preference) and money supply. (4) Keynes suggested the law of diminishing marginal propensity to consume, the law of diminishing marginal efficiency of capital, and the liquidity preference theory. (5) Keynes put forward the multiplier theory, and stated that initial increases in investments can lead to increased induced investments, and through the chain effect, ultimately to effective demand increases in society many times over the initial investments, and vice versa. (6) Keynes put forward a theory of economic cycles, suggesting that an economic cycle mainly consists of four stages: prosperity, depression, recession and recovery, caused by the fluctuations in the investment rate, whilst the fluctuations in the investment rate are due to changes in the capital marginal efficiency. In addition, Keynes studied the price theory, the wage theory, and international trade theory, etc. Thus, Keynes' contribution to the revolution of economic theory, known as the "Keynesian Revolution", is publicly acclaimed as the equivalent of Copernicus' contribution to astronomy, Darwin's to biology, and Einstein's to physics.

Keynes' *General Theory of Employment, Interest and Money* summed up and integrated a large number of economic concepts from a macro perspective, opening a new chapter in the development of economics in the 20th century. The above analyses have shown that: (1) Keynes' unique experiences in academia and politics allowed him to discover a new field in the promotion of national economic growth in the field of public works and public goods investment centered on infrastructure, instead of "foreign trade" advocated by mercantilism, or "agriculture and animal husbandry" advocated by the physiocracy, or the "commodity production sectors" and "industrial economy" of Adam Smith. (2) The government is the primary body in the field of infrastructure investment. To put it another way, the government is the primary body to intervene in the economy and promote economic growth in this field. (3) The main measures of the government in infrastructure investment are fiscal policies rather than monetary policies. Hence, Keynes' economics extended beyond the limits of classical economics and neoclassical economics: On the one hand, classical and neoclassical economics followed the logic of "formation of the commodity price—formation of the industrial economy which centers on the commodity production sectors—persistence of the enterprises as the main body of the free economy—all the main bodies abiding by the market rules" to boost economy. On the other hand, Keynes and the Keynesian school followed the path of "government investment in public projects and public goods— government investment mainly in infrastructure or the development of urban economy—government as the main body of infrastructure investment—government adoption of active fiscal policies" to effectively promote economic growth. From the trajectory of economic growth, it was clear that Keynes and later Keynesians did push the development of economics beyond the limits of product-price analyses, which is the extremely successful and unique contribution of Keynes and Keynesian economics.

However, with the development of Keynesian theories and related government policies, we find some problems. (1) Keynes did not, in basic economics theory, strictly distinguish the public works, public goods and material goods in essence. Instead, he consciously or subconsciously placed public works and public goods into the framework of commodity-price analysis. (2) There were no strict definitions and distinctions between infrastructure and urban economy with material production and industrial economy. In fact, the motives for Keynes to put forward government intervention was to solve the problems of unemployment and economic growth; the government intervened with active fiscal policies and investing large sums of money in public works and public goods centered on infrastructure investment, which belonged to urban economy. Urban economy, as it turned out, had not fully developed during Adam Smith's era. Limitations of the times led to Adam Smith's definition of infrastructure and urban economic development only as public goods, which private investors were unable to get profits from, but could only be provided by the government. In Keynes' times 160 years later (from *The Wealth of Nations* of 1776 to *The General Theory of Employment, Interest and Money* of 1936), although he defined such public works and public goods as a semi-autonomous area between private investors and the state, he did not specifically suggest that these did not belong to industrial economy, but rather, urban economy. Urban economy can be seen in both a broad sense and a narrow sense. In a broad sense, urban economy included not only industrial economy (operational), livelihood economy (non-operational), but also public works and public goods economy which centered on infrastructure investment and development (quasi-operational). In a narrow sense, urban economy referred specifically to public works and public goods economy which centered on infrastructure investment and development. Different from industrial economy, it was but a new economic field, a new resource generation field. Mixing urban economy and industrial economy into one would cause a series of contradictions in economics, especially market economic theories. (3) Keynes did not strictly distinguish between the main participants in urban economy (infrastructure investment) and those in industrial economy. The main participants of commodity production in industrial economy were the industries; whilst the main participants in urban economy (the field of infrastructure investment) would firstly be the government, but at the same time, private investors and alliance investors. Keynes' analysis of effective demand included investment demand and consumption demand, insufficient investment demand resulting from decline in capital marginal efficiency and liquidity preference. The former referred to a decline in return on investment and the latter to preference of people to retain cash. From Keynes' analysis of the decline in investment profit margins, infrastructure investors not only included the government, but also private and alliance investors, as they jointly participated in investment, following the rules and operating mechanism of the market. Derived from this was the concept of "return on investment (ROI)" in urban economy (infrastructure investment), whose participants included the government, private investors and investor union, its operation under market rules in the fields of public works and public goods. However, as Keynes and Keynesian economics did not distinguish between government's participation/intervention in urban economy and enterprises' participation in industrial economy, therefore arose the problem in its economics of the vague roles of the government and industries in industrial economy or market economy. Consequently, there arose a series of theoretical and practical disputes against the so-called "government intervention" by the defenders of classical and neoclassical economics, or the so-called defenders of market economy. (4) To elaborate, Keynes and Keynesian economics did not further clarify whether market rules were limited to the production of commodities in industrial economy, or also included infrastructure investment-centered public works and public goods in urban economy. Thereby, whether governments, as one of the investors, should also follow market rules in the investment of public works and public goods was not clarified. (5) To analyze further, as governments had participated in urban economy—the investment of public works and public goods, were they in competitive relationships with other regional governments, private investors, and alliance investors? How should governments' roles be defined and differentiated in the development of industrial economy and urban economy? Before these questions were effectively solved, having found a new field that can promote national economic growth, Keynes and Keynesian economics then rushed to adopt related policies and measures and study the practical results to help solve problems in this field. They did not address some fundamental economic issues, thereby, resulting in ambiguity and confusion in assumptions and later analyses, and creating an "ambiguous area" which led to endless controversies and contradictions in later generations.

To sum up, (1) Keynes' theory abandoned the support provided by Adam Smith's theories, established its own system with a unique style, but yet consciously or subconsciously relied on the support of Adam Smith's market theory of industrial economy. The key points of Adam Smith's theories included: "selfishness" and "sympathy" integrating to form "an invisible hand" in *The Moral Sentiments*, and "egoism" and "altruism" integrating to form "an invisible hand" in *The Wealth of Nations*. Keynes found a new field that can promote national economic growth—the development and utilization of infrastructure resources and urban resources. However, there was a lack of rational support as far as government functions and roles of a nation were concerned; or perhaps, he had no chance to do the research yet. (2) The regulatory methods of Keynes and the Keynesian school to promote economic growth embodied the principles of balanced supply, effective demand, optimal allocation of resources, and benign economic development, etc. However, the theory did not point out that with the prosperity of the nation and progress of its science and technology, there arose the problem of the development of urban resources and international resources like space resources, deep sea resources and polar resources. In national economic growth, the new subject of new resources and resource generation needed to be further studied. Scarcity and generation of resources are twins in the allocation of resources in economics. (3) The development of economic theories lags behind the changes in economic reality. Keynes adopted Adam Smith's theory on the allocation of industrial resources, but yet did not explore problems on the generation of urban resources/infrastructure resources, thereby considering problems in isolation. Keynesian economics at this time, being practical, prescribed a cure only on the symptoms instead of on the root cause of the problems. In my opinion, this is where the real problem of Keynes' theories lies. (4) The generation and effective allocation of new resources need a system of rules and regulations for support and guarantee. The regulations would help the government, as one of the main subjects in the development and utilization of new resources, determine what to do with the development and utilization of current resources—industrial resources, as well as how to regulate the development and utilization of new resources—urban resources. It was precisely such lack of rules and regulations that had become another weakness in Keynes' theories. (5) The foundation of economic theories is subject to "evolution paradigms". Hence, we should draw lessons and experiences from successful cases of economic practices, learn from the dynamic deductive process history has taught, and use "resource scarcity" and "resource generation" from the core principles of "resource allocation" in economics as a starting point to further analyze and develop modern market theory and modern economics system.

Notes

1. John Maynard Keynes. *The Economic Consequences of the Peace*. New York: Skyhorse Publishing, Inc., 2016, p. 136.
2. John Wasik. "Keynes Answers His Critics", Forbes, May 30, 2013, https://www.forbes.com/sites/johnwasik/2013/05/30/keynes-answers-his-critics/#318b414e2a6b.
3. See "Japanese Experts: Trump's Economic Policies Are like Roosevelt's 'New Deal'", China News, April 1, 2017, http://www.chinanews.com/gj/2017/04-01/8189095.shtml.

Chapter 3
Scarcity and Generation of Resources

1 Scarcity and Generation of Resources Are a Pair of Twins in Resource Allocation

Faced with massive unemployment in Britain in the 1920s and the Great Depression in the United States and even the whole world in the 1930s, the master economist Keynes, with his unique experiences in academia and politics, found an effective solution and discovered a new path and a new field for a country's economic growth, namely, apart from stimulating industrial economy, enhancing effective demand by investing in infrastructure to effectively solve the problem of unemployment and promote a country's economic recovery and growth. However, to implement these measures required the government to be the main body in initiating investment, therefore contradicting Adam Smith's definition of "night watchman state".

Why couldn't Keynes and the subsequent Keynesian school explain and solve this problem under the principles and framework of economics? This required one to start with Adam Smith's *The Wealth of Nations*.

In *The Wealth of Nations*, Adam Smith first put forward two assumptions when discussing economic activities of human society, namely, the egoism of economic activities and resource scarcity. Commodity economy integrates egoism and altruism to form the "invisible hand", forming the system of commodities, prices, demand and supply, and competition, and eventually forming the market rules; resource scarcity leads to a universal rule in the selection of the control target in economy: the optimized allocation of resources and the healthy development of economy. With regard to the two assumptions, the "invisible hand" and the market rules have long become the Bible of classical and neoclassical economics; and "resource allocation" and "resource scarcity" have been taken as the starting point for economic research by both liberal economics and Keynesian economics. Just as P. A. Samuelson said, "Economics is the study of how societies use scarce resources to produce valuable goods and services and distribute them among different individuals."[1]

Y. Chen, *New Economic Engine: Effective Government and Efficient Market*, China Academic Library, https://doi.org/10.1007/978-981-15-2922-1_3

Hence, when traditional economics discusses resource allocation, it cannot escape the association with resource scarcity. Resource allocation is itself defined as the choice made after comparing the various purposes that relatively scarce resources can be used for. According to traditional economics, at a certain stage of social economic development, compared to people's needs, resources tend to be relatively scarce, thereby requiring society to rationally allocate these limited and relatively scarce resources, so as to utilize the least amount of resources to produce the most suitable and useful goods and services, and maximize the benefits. Taking a step further, whether or not resources can be allocated rationally has become an extremely critical factor in determining the success or failure of a country's economic development.

Here, we are neither denying the importance of resource allocation, nor the necessary connection between resource allocation and resource scarcity, nor that the law of resource scarcity has become the starting point for economic research. However, we cannot study resource allocation without discussing, contemplating and exploring the problem of "resource generation". The current situation is quite different from that of Adam Smith's time: (1) When Adam Smith published *The Wealth of Nations* in 1776, the Industrial Revolution just started in Britain. At that time, what Adam Smith referred to as resource allocation was merely the allocation of industrial resources such as people, money and material associated with the production, exchange, and consumption of goods, and not others. (2) The urban infrastructure in Britain around 1776 was still rather backward, consisting of nothing more than roads, bridges, canals and ports. It was inadequate to be used to solve massive unemployment and economic crisis as in Keynes' era more than a hundred years later. (3) The construction of modernized infrastructure we have in modern society involves not only a series of investment projects in hardware and software, but also a series of projects in the development and construction process of intelligent cities. These have become the new field and new resources to promote a country's economic growth, thereby giving rise to the issue of resource generation. This new field of resource generation could be referred to as "urban resources"; different from traditional industrial resources in nature and allocation, they promote economic growth from a different route.

The introduction of urban resources and resource generation is crucial for economics for it can untangle a contradiction in Keynesian theories: finding a new field to promote a country's economic growth on the one hand, and being restricted to using industrial economic ideology to analyze and solve problems on the other. Being a pair of twins in resource allocation theories in economics, resource generation and resource scarcity are two inseparable aspects that are closely related to economic development and progress of the times. Urban resources (needless to say, there will be international resources such as space resources, deep sea resources, polar resources, etc. subsequently) differ from industrial resources that Adam Smith studied during his time, in their nature, contents and functions. Each of them exerts different effects on the economic practice and the theories of economics. We should rectify the situation in traditional economics where there was no research, discussion nor analysis on resource generation, or its effects on economic development and theories of economics. We should abandon traditional economics' habit of merely using the theories and methods of industrial resources allocation to understand, contemplate, and explain the effects of the new-born resource generation, which emphasized efficient allocation of resources based only on resource scarcity and discussed merely equilibrium and disequilibrium in distributions. These resulted in the economic theories' development deviating from reality or lagging behind changes in economic reality, leaving resource generation and its corresponding institutional construction and regulation setting void. These are the problems we should solve at the moment.

2 From Resource Generation to Generative Resources

Generative resources, generated from "resource generation", featured as dynamic, economic and productive, are economic resources like industrial resources.

Resource generation is not arising out of plan, but rather pre-exists or arises from the objective needs of the times. It becomes dynamic when it can be produced to generate revenue. A mountain which sits idle, as an example, is a static natural resource, but once developed into a dynamic production factor, it becomes an important economic resource. Land, mines, water, forests, grasslands, and other static landscapes are natural resources; once developed, they become economic resources; this is a fact long known to all. Urban infrastructure—hardware, software, and development and construction of intelligent cities—is to cater for the objective needs of the times, and possesses the characteristics of resource generation. It is another generative resource following industrial resources—urban resources. Of course, there are space resources which are similar (there are actually many more usable resources in outer space than on earth). Just within the solar system, there are vast deposits of mineral resources on celestial bodies such as the Moon, Mars and other asteroids; on Jovian planets and the comet, there is an abundance of hydrogen energy; in planetary and interplanetary spaces, there exist vacuum resources, radioactive resources and vast temperature difference resources; furthermore, through flights of spacecraft, orbital resources, micro-gravity resources and others can be generated. In their static states, these are natural resources, but once developed and utilized, they become productive factors, and are important and treasured economic resources. With regard to the generation, development and utilization of such resources, can national governments not play a role as one of the subjects? Can we still explain and promote it only using traditional theories of industrial economy? Obviously not. In reality, the government plays a different role in the generation, development and utilization of urban resources from what it plays in the development of industrial economy.

Urban resources can be defined in a broad and a narrow sense.

Firstly, cities are not randomly built, most of which are gradually formed in the process of historical development. Secondly, cities are neither static nor fixed; most of them gradually expand through dynamic interactions. Furthermore, cities are not single-functional. Most of them include the functions of hardware and software infrastructure, and even modernized intelligent cities in a three-dimensional development pattern. All the conditions on which the building, existence and development of cities depend are deemed as urban resources.

Hence, from an economic perspective, urban resources in a broad sense contain industrial resources, livelihood resources, and infrastructure resources or public works resources. Urban resources in a narrow sense are what we will discuss at length: Why did Keynes find a new field to boost the economic growth of a nation, but couldn't explain it by price theory and industrial economic theory? Why did the previous Roosevelt Administration or the incumbent Trump Administration invest in infrastructure construction in their attempt to solve economic depression and promote economic growth? (Infrastructure construction has become a measure pursued globally to promote economic growth; for instance, China has invested in infrastructure construction of "Belt and Road" nations.) These questions could be answered by the research into urban resources in their narrow sense. As important generative resources, urban resources in their narrow sense include investment and construction of hardware and software infrastructure, as well as the development and operation of intelligent cities in the process of further modernization. It is a new economic field whose theories are worth developing, whose market rules are worth exploring, whose government-market relationship is worth studying to discover a new engine for national and even global economy. It is related to and different from theories of industrial economics. Modern economists really should not just rely on theories of industrial economics to explain or promote the development of urban economy and urban resources.

Urban infrastructure, as generative resources, refers to public work facilities that provide public services for social production and residents' living, and is a public goods system to ensure smooth running of national and regional social economic activities and residents' daily lives. It includes not only hardware public facilities such as roads, railways, airports, communications, water, electricity, gas and others, but also software public services such as education, science and technology, health care, sports, culture and others. With the progress of urban modernization, it also includes the series of development and construction of intelligent cities. To put it in detail, hardware mainly refers to the six major systematic engineering infrastructure: (1) energy supply system, such as electricity, gas, natural gas, liquefied petroleum gas, heating, etc.; (2) water supply and drainage system, such as water resource protection, water plants, water distribution system, drainage and sewerage; (3) transportation system, divided into external transport facilities (e.g., aviation, railways, shipping, coaches and highways) and internal ones (e.g., roads, bridges, tunnels, subways, light rails, public transportation, taxis, parking facilities, and ferries); (4) posts and telecommunications system, such as postal service, telegraphs, landline phones, mobile phones, internet, radio and television, etc.; (5) environmental protection and sanitation system, such as landscaping, garbage collection and disposal, pollution control, etc.; (6) defense and disaster prevention safety system, for disasters such as fire, flood, earthquake, typhoon, sand storm, ground subsidence, air defense, etc. Software mainly refers to administrative management, culture and education, health care, commercial services, financial insurance, social welfare, and other infrastructure for social services. With the progress of urban-rural integration, software also includes four main types, namely infrastructure for rural production, rural daily living, construction of ecological environment, and rural social development. With the progress of urban modernization, the development and construction of intelligent cities has become a new part of urban infrastructure. The urban infrastructure, as new generative resources, are fundamental, non-trading and quasi-public goods in economics, become a new field that could promote national economic development and open a new path to reforming economics theories.

3 Three Types of Resources in Cities

Back to reality, the 21st century is a century marked by the co-existence and co-prosperity of economic development, urban construction, and social livelihood. In practice, governments manifest their economic functions through the allocation and management of various resources. In other words, governments would classify from an economic perspective natural resources, human resources, capital resources, industrial resources, urban resources, and public goods resources that exist in reality within their territories, optimize their allocation, and make parallel policies. There are three major resources in cities:

(1) Resources that relate to economic development, otherwise known as "operational resources" in market economy, are mainly industrial resources in regional economy in various countries. As the economic geographical and natural conditions differ, regions would choose one from the primary industry, secondary industry, and tertiary industry as the lead in their economic development. In reality, needless to say, in the process of the development of the primary and secondary sectors, there have been numerous cases of successful development of the tertiary sector, such as logistics, exhibition, finance, tourism, intermediary service, and retail trade. In traditional economics, companies and enterprises are related to these resources, or in other words, are the main bodies in the development of industrial economy. There are three types of governmental institutions in China that coordinate, monitor, and manage such resources: (i) development and reform, statistics and prices; (ii) (a) treasury, finance, taxation, industry and commerce; (b) industry, transport, security, energy and tobacco; (c) science and technology, information, private communications, intellectual property rights; (d) commerce, customs, maritime affairs, ports, postal service, quality inspection, foreign affairs, tourism; (iii) audit, territorial supervision, food and pharmaceutical supervision and management, etc. The governmental institutions of coordinating, supervising and managing may be similar or different across different nations, but they share the main principles of "invigoration" in resource allocation; that is, to plan and guide, to support and coordinate, to supervise and manage. This is already commonly agreed upon in theory.

(2) Resources that relate to social livelihood, otherwise known as "non-operational resources" in market economy, are mainly the social welfare and public goods in various regions, including economy (guarantee), history, geography, image, spirit, idea, emergency, security, relief and other social needs in regions. In traditional economics, the government and social enterprises are related to these resources, to put it another way, are the main organizations in the provision of social welfare and public goods. The governmental institutions in China that coordinate, monitor, and manage such resources are: (i) (a) finance, audit, public sectors; (b) literature and history, counseling, archives; (c) civil affairs, social security, poverty alleviation; (d) women and children, Federation of Disabled Persons, the Red Cross, etc.; (e) ethnic groups, religions, overseas Chinese affairs; (ii) geology, earthquake, meteorology; (iii) (a) emergency, safety and security, air defense; (b) people's armed forces, public security, judiciary, supervision organs; (c) fire brigade, armed police, border defense, coast guards and anti-smuggling, etc. Similar governmental institutions may have different names in different nations, but they share the main principles of resource allocation, namely, "social guarantee, general underpinning; fairness and justice, effective promotion". This is also consistent in practice and cognition.

(3) Resources that relate to urban construction, otherwise known as "quasi-operational resources" in market economy, are mainly the urban resources across various regions. These are mainly public service systems to ensure the smooth running of national or regional social economic activities, the software and hardware infrastructure to provide public service for social production and residents' daily living, namely the urban infrastructure described above in "resource generation", including transportation, posts and telecommunications, power and water supply, landscaping, environmental protection, education, science and technology, culture, health, sports and other urban public works and public life service facilities. The quality of the software and hardware infrastructure directly affects the appearance, characteristics, taste, functions and effects of a nation or region. The completeness of the software and hardware infrastructure shall promote the development of social, economic and other undertakings across nations and regions, and push the optimization of urban spatial distribution and structure. The reason why I classify these resources as quasi-operational resources is that they don't have clear definitions in traditional economics. They belong to the "cross-over region" between the government and enterprises, that is, the investment and development of urban infrastructure, as an undertaking to promote economic development and social livelihood, can be undertaken by either enterprises or the government. The governmental institutions in China that coordinate, monitor, and manage such resources are: (i) state-owned assets, major projects; (ii) land resources, environmental protection, urban and rural construction; (iii) human resources, public resource transactions; (iv) education, science and technology, culture, health, sports, press and publication, radio, film and television, research institutions, etc.; (v) agriculture, forestry, water conservation, marine fisheries, etc. The urban quasi-operational resources are the

basis for investigating resource generation and investment in infrastructure, and deepening the economic theory analysis.

Theories and practices have taught us: (1) Pertaining to operational resources—industrial resources and industrial economy, resources should be allocated by the market to enterprises, society and various domestic and foreign investors by taking capitalization measures as much as possible. Governments should then design their policies in accordance with the principles of "planning and guidance, support and coordination, supervision and management". (2) Pertaining to non-operational resources—public goods and livelihood economy, in other words, in areas out of reach of enterprises, governments should be responsible for the supply, allocation, management and development of such resources in all facets, and design governmental policies following the principles of "fairness and justice, general underpinning, effective promotion". This is the reason why the national treasury, which is derived from and to be used by the public, should weaken its constructive treasury functions and instead, strengthen its public (public benefits) treasury functions. (3) Pertaining to quasi-operational resources—(narrowly defined as) urban resources and urban economy, governments should determine whether these are to be developed and allocated as operational resources or to be operated and managed as public welfare undertakings, depending upon the direction of regional development, treasury status, capital flows, demand of enterprises and the acceptability and affordability of the public amongst other reasons.

4 The Investment Entities of Urban Infrastructure

The investment, development, and management of urban infrastructure, i.e. quasi-operational resources, present problems in its implementation across various nations: that of determining the investment carrier and of operating the investment fund.

(1) Pertaining to the problem of determining the investment carrier—if we put the urban infrastructure, i.e. quasi-operational resources, into the market system for its investment, development, operation and management, then, governments can set up the carrier of urban infrastructure construction projects through sole proprietorships, joint ventures, cooperation, shareholding systems and even state-owned but privately-operated enterprises. Such equity structures, in accordance with market demand, social supply and objective trends of domestic and international economic development, can not only finance effectively, optimize structure, stabilize economic and social development, but also effectively regulate and control the market according to forecast, and avoid massive losses by preventing certain regional governments from problems in the construction and development of urban infrastructure. The problems include huge wastes of urban resources, wasteful repeated construction of urban infrastructure, low-level, low-standard and disorderly operation of urban economic management. These

problems arise from certain regional governments providing for society public goods for free service and sharing; investing without profiting; constructing without managing and operating; focusing on social benefits only but ignoring economic benefits. Hence, during the selection of the investment, development, operation and management methods of urban infrastructure (quasi-operational resources), regional governments across the world should, with regard to existing urban infrastructure resources, reform the ownership structure of "stock assets" carriers, and build up and operate carriers adaptable to capital market financing means according to market rules and objective demands of economic development; in other words, they could transform the "stock assets" carriers into state-owned but privately-run, shareholding, joint venture, cooperation forms, or auction off to investors home and abroad to operate and manage, making them equity carriers which conform to market economy rules and participate in market competition. With regard to newly added urban infrastructure projects, or "incremental assets", governments should organize the platform carriers in sole proprietorship, joint venture, cooperation or share-holding forms right from the beginning, and lay the foundation for equity carriers and their development conditions according to market rules, thus turning them into participants in the competition for resource investment, urban development and operation. Steps need to be taken to avoid returning to the old path where government is the sole equity investor in the investment, development, and operation of incremental assets.

(2) Pertaining to the problem of the operation of investment funds—if we invest, develop, operate and manage the urban infrastructure (quasi-operational resources) in the market system, regional governments across the world can solve the problem by capital market financing, for example, issuing bonds or convertible bonds, issuing stocks, setting up project funds or utilizing investment projects by local and foreign funds, back-door listing projects as entities, securitization of project assets, project merger and acquisition, leasing, mortgage, swaps, auction, etc. Governments can also make use of charging and pricing power and use DBO (design-build-operate), BOT (build-operate-transfer), BOO (build-operate-own), BOOT (build-operate-own-transfer), BLT (build-lease-transfer), BTO (build-transfer-operate), TOT (transfer-operate-transfer), amongst others, to implement the capital operation of franchise rights. Governments can also implement or alternately implement different capital operations, according to the different characteristics and conditions of quasi-operational resources, i.e., infrastructure projects—such as using the "PPP" (public-private partnership) model to build equity carriers, or using "PPC" (port-park-city) as a development model to create a rather perfect infrastructure investment and construction economic circle integrating infrastructure, logistics, finance and industrial park facilities. Utilizing BOT, TOT, or other ways to exercise franchising rights, and as conditions mature, the project company can be transformed into a publicly listed company. Through the issuance of stocks or bonds, urban infrastructure projects can be further strengthened and expanded, thereby

helping regional governments to overcome their capital bottleneck, enhancing the investment, development, operation, and management of urban infrastructure, and achieving scientific and sustainable development. The effects of the limited public finances would be multiplied, more effectively satisfying the ever increasing demand of the public on public goods and public welfare undertakings.

To sum up, in the process of the investment, development, operation and management of quasi-operational resources, namely, urban infrastructure, the mode of "government promotion, enterprise participation and market-based operation" implies the following three principles from the beginning—(1) regional governments are one of the main competition subjects in urban economy; (2) regional governments should and must rely on market rules and act according to market regulations in the investment, development, operation and management in this field; (3) at the same time, regional governments are also the national representatives in the investment, development, operation and management thereof, taking on the functions of guiding, coordinating and supervising. Hence, for the investment, development, operation and management of quasi-operational resources or urban infrastructure, governments should follow the above-mentioned principles to design their policies.

Note

1. Paul A. Samuelson and William D. Nordhaus. *Economics*. New York: McGraw-Hill/Irwin, 2010, p. 4.

Chapter 4
The Dual Attributes of Government

1 The Three Functions of Regional Governments

There are two fatal deficiencies in traditional economic market theory, namely that government, market, and society are independent bodies, and government has always been placed out of the market ever since the era of Adam Smith; and that the functions of government are single and restricted to those of public affairs and the provision of public goods and services to society and the public, and do not involve promoting economic development or competing in urban infrastructure construction. These theories have seriously restricted the performance of regional governments' functions across the world.

Maintaining stability, promoting development, and handling emergencies are the three basic duties of governments throughout the world.

Through surveying regional governments across the world, economic development, urban construction, and social livelihood are deemed as the three main economic functions. Regional governments at all levels making diligent efforts to explore and playing positive roles during the process of China's reform and opening up are such an example.

Firstly, regarding economic development, many regional governments have made fruitful exploration. In as early as 2005, Shunde District in Foshan City, Guangdong Province, China, achieved a regional GDP of 60.1 billion RMB, the secondary industry accounting for 61%, among which household appliances and household electronics accounted for 70% of total industrial output, with the household electrical appliance industry mainly dominated by the three giants Midea, Kelon, and Galanz. Faced with this situation, to prevent the risk of regional economic crisis brought about by mismanagement in certain enterprises in a single industry, the Shunde government, based on practice, scientifically put forward and implemented a "Triple-Three Strategy" for its industrial development, that is, to guide and support the coordinated development of the primary, secondary, and tertiary industries; within each industry, to guide and support more than three pillar industries; within

Y. Chen, *New Economic Engine: Effective Government and Efficient Market*, China Academic Library, https://doi.org/10.1007/978-981-15-2922-1_4

each pillar industry, to guide and support more than three leading enterprises; to perfect the industrial chain, form industrial clusters, and promote sustainable development.[1] Faced with problems of weak foundation and shortage of funds during the growth of a large number of medium-sized, small, and microenterprises, the Shunde government innovated and set up a credit guarantee fund for medium-sized, small, and microenterprises. The regional government arranged special quota funds and cooperated with professional guarantee agencies and commercial banks to provide guarantee and loans to growing medium-sized, small, and microenterprises which would otherwise have problems securing loans from banks due to a lack of collateral.[2] It has been proved that the Shunde government's guidance, regulation, and forewarning in the economic field have promoted the fine development of the primary industry, optimum development of the secondary industry, and accelerated development of the tertiary industry; promoted the transformation and upgrading of traditional industries, the growth of emerging industries, and the rapid growth of high-tech industries; and formed a situation where big, medium-sized, and small industries developed in gradient, and industrial clusters complemented one another. Shunde has managed to maintain its leading position till this day among over 2,800 counties in China.

Western developed nations are also stepping up their efforts to guide, promote, and regulate the development of the industrial economy. The National Network for Manufacturing Innovation (NNMI) is one of the US government's most important measures to reindustrialize the country. Following the international financial crisis, the USA announced "A Framework for Revitalizing American Manufacturing," passed the United States Manufacturing Enhancement Act of 2010, and launched the Advanced Manufacturing Partnership (AMP) in June 2011. And in March 2012, the National Network for Manufacturing Innovation was launched, with responsibilities held by various mutually related Institutes for Manufacturing Innovation (IMIs),[3] which have common goals with respective focuses. The USA invested a total of 1 billion US dollars to establish 15 IMIs across the nation, and further in July 2013, proposed that within 10 years, the target was to establish 45 IMIs, and included and implemented the proposal in the budget for the fiscal year 2015. The NNMI has the following main characteristics. Firstly, guided by national strategic objectives and in accordance with regional and industrial needs, it organized research and development projects relatively independently. Secondly, with resource optimization and redistribution as its core, it combined "top-down" and "bottom-up" measures to carry out the integration of existing innovative resources. Thirdly, it was guaranteed by public and private cooperation. The federal government shall provide relatively stable support during the early stages, followed up by supporting funds and other packages from universities, private organizations, and others. Fourthly, supported by network governance, each IMI linked regional, federal, and international innovative resources, and through the establishment of a leadership council, NNMI promoted coordination and cooperation between IMIs. Henceforth, in the connection of the government with the market, in the process to optimize government investment and coordinate multi-stakeholder relationships, the government demonstrated its investment guidance functions, realized the leverage effects, led the direction for research and development in industries, promoted the layout for high-end manufacturing, and accelerated innovation and commercialization.

Apart from the US, the United Kingdom's Knowledge Transfer Partnership (KTP) scheme is also noteworthy. The plan was launched in 2003. By supporting the partnership between businesses and academic organizations, with talents with certain knowledge and technological skills as the media, the transfer of knowledge, technology, and skills from research organizations to businesses was realized, thereby helping businesses elevate their innovation capabilities. KTP's funds not only came from the public funds of government and public organizations, but also from supporting funds of businesses. KTP established the application criteria and approval protocol for funds and an implementation and acceptance evaluation system. KTP expanded the services provided to businesses, prompted businesses' innovative investments, integrated innovative resources from talents, businesses and organizations, and promoted the upgrading and development of the industrial structure.

Secondly, regarding urban construction, regional governments have a lot to do. By 2006, Foshan City, Guangdong Province of China, riding on the strength of the reform and opening up policy, used a threefold increase in land use for construction to achieve a 30-fold increase in economic growth. However, at the same time, Foshan also faced the grim reality of an obvious disequilibrium between land supply and demand, which had become the main bottleneck stifling the future development of the city. With the unrelenting efforts in practice by the Foshan government, in 2007, the "Provisions Regarding the Acceleration of Transformation of Outmoded Towns, Outmoded Factory Buildings and Outmoded Villages" was promulgated (abbreviated as "The Three-Outmoded Transformation"). In 2009, the "Foshan Special Plan for the Three-Outmoded Transformation (2009–2020)" was promulgated, and the city's "Three-Outmoded Transformation" land, covering an area of 253,000 mu (168.67 million square meters), was formally released to be utilized in adherence to the market reform model of "the government setting policies, owners (users) contributing land, and developers contributing capital." Within the first three years, 35.7 billion RMB was successfully introduced, 730 "Three-Outmoded Transformation" projects were launched, covering an area of approximately 30,000 mu (20 million square meters), and added a total area of 23.99 million square meters of new buildings. The "Three-Outmoded Transformation" characterized by "government facilitation, market operation, and enterprise participation" rapidly improved the regional construction, greatly enhanced the efficiency of land use, and at the same time promoted the adjustment and improvement in the structures of land use and industries. This was acclaimed and popularized by Guangdong and the rest of the nation as the "Foshan Experience."[4] Following closely behind in 2010, the Foshan government put forward a development plan of "Integration of Informatization, Industrialization, Urbanization, and Internationalization for an Intelligent Foshan." This involved the use of information technology to promote industrialization, urbanization, and internationalization, to enhance the overall competitiveness of Foshan. Through vigorous development of intelligent transportation, intelligent environmental protection, intelligent land monitoring, intelligent public security, intelligent urban management, intelligent education, intelligent medical treatment, intelligent culture, intelligent commerce, intelligent government affairs, etc., the goal of urban security, efficiency, convenience, green, and harmony was fully attained by the Foshan government, thereby promoting the transition of regional industrialization, accelerating the process of urbanization and furthering its internationalization.[5]

During the process of modernization of urban governance, the government plays an important role. This is also an unavoidable topic in Western developed nations. The nirvana of Germany's "Industrial Toxic Capital," the Ruhr Industrial Zone, is an example. While bringing Germany's massive economic contributions, it has, at the same time, created massive pollution. To combat pollution, the Nordrhein-Westfalen and German government formulated an outline. From 1968 to 1979, and then to 1989, came a long "trilogy": the adjustment of industrial structure, the development of new industries, and ecological revamp, repair, and environmental improvement of the industrial heritage. The Ruhr industrial zone finally attained jointly the inheritance of regional culture, industrial transformation and upgrading, infrastructure transformation, and urban development. The old industrial zone has become a modern-styled urban industrial zone suitable again for living, commerce, and development.

Finally, regarding social livelihood, the government is duty-bound. In 2016, for example, the Guangdong Provincial Government of China put forward ten things to do that can bring real benefits to people: (1) to strengthen the capability to meet basic needs; (2) to enhance the level of support for disadvantaged groups; (3) to strengthen housing security for the low-income groups who have housing difficulties; (4) to improve the living and production conditions in rural areas; (5) to improve basic medical and health services; (6) to promote fair and equitable distribution of educational resources; (7) to promote entrepreneurship and employment; (8) to strengthen pollution control and management, and ecological construction; (9) to strengthen public security; (10) to prevent and mitigate disasters.[6] Each item was concrete and down-to-earth.

Beginning in the 1970s, the "New Village Movement" in the ROK is another classic example. Faced with the situation that farmers accounted for 70% of the population and that agriculture was on the verge of collapse, the ROK government proposed to launch the New Village Movement to revitalize agriculture. The government made policies and provided goods and materials to facilitate rural construction projects, support the National Agriculture Cooperative Federation (NACF) to establish and run their own cooperative finance, spared no effort to push forward the movement, created the renowned "Han River Miracle," and realized enormous growth in the economy. The ROK's experience has set an example for solving the problems of livelihood in a country, especially where there are serious urban and rural imbalances.

2 The Dual Roles of Regional Governments

The three major economic functions of regional governments as described above are essentially the three major missions of governments in governing their regional economies; or from an economics viewpoint, a management or policy arrangement by which governments manage the three types of economic matters in their respective regions; or as it can be said, an allocation or optimization of the three types of economic resources in their respective regions. In any case, to realize these three economic functions, the government needs to make relevant policies, in order to achieve the best economic development and social stability at the least cost, help the nation achieve prosperity and strength, and the public live and work in peace and contentment.

As has been analyzed earlier, with regard to the operational resources, which is industrial economy, or traditional market-operated field, regional governments should follow the principles of "guidance, coordination, and supervision" to make policies. With regard to the non-operational resources, which are public goods, or social public welfare undertakings, regional governments should follow the principles of "general underpinning, fairness and justice, and effective promotion" to make policies. With regard to the quasi-operational resources, namely urban infrastructure, which belong to "ambiguous areas," or "overlapping areas" in the traditional market theory system, this is precisely the point where we might achieve breakthroughs in traditional economics system or traditional governmental governance. The economies in various nations have proceeded from the "factor-driven" to the "investment-driven" stages and are currently progressing toward the new "innovation-driven" stage. The various problems that have arisen in the current economic operation are not fully manifested as "market failure" or "government failure," but are demonstrated more as deficiencies in traditional economics system or traditional market theory, and the void in modern economics system or the modern market theory.

To realize the three main economic functions as described above, regional governments ought to excel in dual functions.

Firstly, regional governments play the "quasi-enterprise" or "quasi-micro" roles. The planning, guidance, and support of operational resources, that is, industrial economy, by regional governments, and their participation and competition in quasi-operational resources, that is, urban infrastructure investment and operation, have led them to become the centralized agency of non-governmental bodies within the region. Through the innovation of values, institutions, organizations, technologies, and other methods, a region competes with other regions to realize maximum regional economic benefits. As such, regional governments are playing the "quasi-enterprise" and "quasi-micro" role. On the one hand, regional governments and enterprises manifest differences in behavioral purposes, development modes, regulatory factors, and assessment criteria. But on the other hand, both regional governments and enterprises are resource allocators in certain categories, within which they exercise internal management. Competitive mechanism between different regional governments and between enterprises persists and becomes the driving force for the development of both the nation and enterprises; their actions in the industrial economy must adhere to the rules of the market economy—at this point, the regional governments' regional jurisdictions shift toward regional management rights. They allocate resources to maximize regional benefits, with a focus on the solicitation of investment, development, investment, operation, and management of urban infrastructure projects. Regional governments' actions are subject to both political and economic constraints;

regional governments' effectiveness can elevate the region's competitive advantage and complete the region's economic transition and social transformation in advance. To sum up, "quasi" means "not belonging to a certain category, but to a certain extent, possessing certain attributes or functions of this category." Regional governments are not enterprises, but to a certain extent, possess characteristics of enterprises. Consequently, regional governments simultaneously take on certain "quasi-enterprise" and "quasi-micro" roles.

Secondly, regional governments play the "quasi-national" or "quasi-macro" roles. The regulation, supervision, and management of operational resources, that is, industrial economy, by regional governments and their allocation of non-operational resources, that is, public goods or public welfare undertakings under the principles of "general underpinning, fairness and justice, and effective promotion," qualify them to be centralized agencies of national government in their local regions. Regional governments regulate the economy through the means of planning, investment, and consumption, and the systems of price, taxation, interest rate, exchange rate, and law, while maintaining social stability through the provision of a basic social guarantee, public service, etc. As such, regional governments are playing the "quasi-national" or "quasi-macro" roles. As agents of the national government, regional governments, with the publicness and force bestowed on them, perform the political, economic, urban, social, and other functions of their regions. On economic development and urban construction, regional governments are charged with the responsibilities of studying and formulating the medium- and long-term plans for regional economic and social development; promoting the dynamic balance between aggregate supply and aggregate demand in the region; implementing national economic policies; formulating regional industrial and technical policies; investing vigorously in infrastructure construction; providing public goods and services; effectively adjusting income distribution and redistribution; while maintaining regional aggregate economic growth, structural dynamic equilibrium, and effective urban upgrading, upholding at the same time regional market rules and order, regulating prices, controlling unemployment rates, and promoting harmonious and sustainable development of society. In practice, regional governments' "quasi-national" or "quasi-macro" roles manifest mainly in the fiscal revenue and expenditure activities. On the revenue side, regional governments use treasury revenue from tax collection, transfer payments, equity, and others to maintain their own operation and perform various functions. On the expenditure side, it mainly includes the following: social consumption expenditures by fiscal purchases, including administration management expenses, national defense security expenses, science, education, culture and health service expenses, as well as industry, transportation, commerce, agriculture, and other departmental expenses; fiscal investment expenditures by governmental investment, including infrastructure investment, scientific and technological research development investment, and policy-based financial investment (to support industries in urgent need of development) and others; and transfer expenditures mainly on the provision of social security, treasury subsidy, and others. Social consumption and treasury investment expenditures, being purchase expenditures, directly affect the allocation of social resources and various factors; their scale and structure roughly demonstrate the strength and scope of regional governments' direct involvement in resource allocation and reflect regional governments' ability to directly regulate social resources within a period of time and the degree of their influence on social economy and others. Transfer expenditures, on the other hand, indirectly affect the allocation of social resources and various factors and assist the implementation of social equity policies.[7]

Finally, the dual roles of regional governments are dialectically unified. The concept of "region" is a relative one. As far as the world is concerned, every nation is a "region." As far as a nation is concerned, every city is a "region." The dual roles of regional governments in each nation have their own inherent attributes: Firstly, governments' institutional supply, which includes the provision of governmental policies, laws, and others, aims at ensuring various public goods and social benefits services are fairly, justly, and effectively put into place. Secondly, governments' economic regulation, which includes governments' support for industrial development, investment in urban infrastructure construction, and others, aims to effectively guide the transformation and upgrading of industries and the urban modernization, to promote scientific, coordinated, and sustainable economic and social progress in the region. So to speak, the dual roles of regional governments are dialectically unified. It is precisely the dual roles that amend the deficiencies of traditional economics system or traditional market theory and open a new chapter on the modern economics system and the modern market theory. Modern market theory tells us that enterprises are the main market competitors in the industrial economy, whereas regional governments are the main market competitors in the urban economy. The development of modern economics system has revealed that apart from microeconomics, which has enterprises as object of study, and macroeconomics, which has the nation or the world as object of study, there should also be mezzoeconomics, which has regional governments as object of study.

3 The Dual Competitors in Market Competition

From the above analysis, we can see that:

Firstly, there are external possibilities for regional governments to participate in the competition. As already known, the publicness of regional governments' management functions is mainly manifested through taxation, industry and commerce, public security, and other supervision measures, which are necessary for guaranteeing regional public expenditure and maintaining regional market and social stability; and their openness, fairness, and justice are ensured by legislation, judiciary, administration, and other means. The regional governments' mandatory management functions are mainly manifested through the three super-economic mandatory powers of legislation, judiciary, and administration, as well as the economic mandatory power to control over money and affairs. From the outside, it appears that regional governments' management functions are manifested through the three main economic areas of economic development, urban construction, and social livelihood; however, in essence, these management functions are the effectiveness of regional governments' allocation of various tangible and intangible resources the regions already or may potentially possess. The management practice across the world and the success of China's reform and opening up have already told us that regional governments should first ensure that the provision of regional social benefits services and public goods meets the standards of "general underpinning, fairness and justice, and effective promotion." On this basis, in order to prevent urban resources, especially urban infrastructure from laying idle and wasted, or large-scale damage of infrastructure, poor quality of urban construction, and disorderly urban management due to investing without profiting, constructing without managing and operating, and focusing only on public benefits and neglecting economic returns, regional governments, through market mechanism, would in part or a majority of areas invest, develop, and manage urban infrastructure—known as quasi-operational resources. In the process of transforming quasi-operational resources into operational resources, the carrier of urban infrastructure investment—the equity nature and structure of infrastructure project companies (e.g., sole proprietorships, joint ventures, partnerships, jointstock companies, even state-owned privately run enterprises, and others) must be set to comply with market rules and regulations; the financial management of urban infrastructure investment, whether through BOT, PPP, or other franchised means, or through public listing and issuance of bonds or stocks to expand and consolidate the infrastructure construction projects, must go through market competition. From the very beginning, the method of "government promotion, enterprise participation, and market operation" has bestowed regional governments with external possibilities to participate in urban economic construction and development competition.

Secondly, regional governments' participation in the competition is inherently inevitable. On the one hand, regional governments' implementation of "general underpinning, fairness and justice, and effective promotion" policies on non-operational resources, that is, public goods or social benefits undertakings and "coordination, supervision, and management" policies on operational resources, that is, industrial economy, lead regional governments to become centralized agents for national government in their respective regions. Regional governments maintain stability through basic social guarantee, public services, and other measures and coordinate the economy through planning, investment, consumption, price, taxation, interest rate, exchange rate, law, and other means. In practice, regional governments mainly utilize treasury revenues and expenditures to realize its publicness and mandatory power. At this point, regional governments play the "quasi-national" and "quasi-macro" roles. On the other hand, regional governments' participation and competition in the investment and operation of quasi-operational resources, that is, urban infrastructure, and planning, guidance, and support of operational resources, that is, industrial economy, lead regional governments to become centralized agents for non-governmental bodies in their regions. Regional governments compete with each other through various innovative measures, carry out resource allocation for the maximization of regional benefits, with emphasis on attracting investment, developing, investing, operating, and managing urban infrastructure construction projects. Regional governments, like enterprises, are the resource allocators and participants within a certain category (urban economy or industrial economy), market competition mechanism being the driving force for development, market rules being the code of conduct they must adhere to. Consequently, at this point, regional governments are playing the "quasi-enterprise" and "quasi-micro" roles. Regional governments' dual roles and the competitive forces arising as a result profoundly indicate that regional governments' participation in the competition is inherently inevitable.

Finally, there exist dual competitors in market competition. Through the analysis of the economic activities of the regional governments, we can reposition the three types of economic functions of the regional governments, distinguish the allocation means of the three regional resources in economics, effectively affirm the different positions of governments and enterprises in urban or industrial economy, and explore and study the dual roles and special effects of regional governments at the microeconomic and macroeconomic levels, which will compose a new chapter in the development of the modern market economy theory: Firstly, there is the aforementioned theory on the dual roles of regional governments. Secondly, note the theory on dual competitors in market competition. On the one hand, the dual-competitor theory clarifies the existence in the modern market system of two competitors, namely enterprises and regional governments. On the other hand, it also tells us that regional governments' competition is mainly concentrated in the investment, development, operation, and management of urban infrastructure, that is, in the competition for various tangible and intangible resources in urban economic development. Its objective is mainly to optimize the allocation of urban resources of the regions and enhance urban economic efficiency and rates of return, and the policies and measures revolve mainly around the leading edges and sustainable development of regional urban economy. There is basically no competition between enterprises and regional governments in the industrial economy as enterprises compete mainly in the industrial economy while regional governments compete mainly in urban economy. Enterprise competition and government competition each occurs in different fields, and together they constitute the dual competitors in the modern market economic system, coexisting and complementing each other. Thirdly, note the theory of "strong-strong mechanism" in a mature market economy, which comprises a strong effective government and a strong efficient market. In the modern market economy theory, we need not only a "strong market," where the market determines the allocation of resources in the industrial economy and urban economy, and the market rules and regulations have fundamental effects on competition therein; but also a "strong government," that is, the regional government is one of the main competitors in urban economy, who relies on and acts in accordance with market rules and regulations, and at the same time needs to plan, guide, support, regulate, supervise, and manage the industrial economy because of its dual roles. A strong-strong mechanism integrating strong effective government and strong efficient market is the real mature mechanism that develops in practice. A modern market mechanism should not just focus on the promotion and development of industrial economy, but also on the allocation of resources, regional competitive forces, and regional sustainable development in urban economy. Together they construct a complete system of the modern market economy and guide the development of economic practices and the progress of economic theories across the world.

4 Thoughts from Three Case Studies

The following are three cases cited in my research on whether various nations across the world need to explore or implement top-level arrangement of national finance, which are not necessarily related to the content of this chapter on "dual attributes of government." Nevertheless, from another perspective, that of monetary and financial competition among nations in the global economy, it incites thoughts on why the US government, while advocating liberal economy in theory, interferes frequently and proactively takes the lead in global economic system competition, resulting in their current status in the world economy. What does this imply?

The first case is the US monetary and financial system established by Alexander Hamilton. Hamilton was the first US Treasury Secretary from 1789 to 1795. During his tenure, Hamilton advocated rebuilding the national credit destroyed in the war, improving the financial system, establishing a complete financial management system, and creating favorable conditions for the development of industry and commerce, hence building the five pillars of the US monetary and financial system: a unified government bond market, a central bank-led banking system, a unified mintage system (gold and silver bimetallism), a tax collection system based mainly on tariff and consumption tax, and financial and trade policies to encourage the development of the manufacturing industry. They have become the solid foundation upon which the modern monetary and financial system of the USA is built, which in turn ultimately leads to the global economy.[8] On this matter, we need to consider.

Why did Hamilton's "financial thinking" over 200 years ago already emphasize so heavily on "national credit"? Why did he think that for the USA to become a prosperous and powerful country, it must have a solid confederation of states and a strong central government? Why do contemporaries regard Hamilton as the greatest Treasury Secretary in American history?

The second case is the international financial system established on the Bretton Woods Conference. In July 1944, the Bretton Woods Conference was convened in New Hampshire, USA. John Maynard Keynes, the then head of the British delegation, put forward a plan for the world financial system before the meeting, that is, a world unit of currency (the bancor), a world central bank, and the International Clearing Union. Harry Dexter White, chief economist of the US Treasury and chairman of the conference representing the USA, on the other hand, in light of the logic that political power takes precedence over economy, adopted political and diplomatic measures at crucial stages of the conference, which eventually led to the establishment of three working committees revolving around their political objectives, discussing, respectively, the International Stability Fund, the International Bank for Reconstruction and Development, and other issues on International Financial Cooperation. Subsequently, the International Monetary Fund (IMF), the World Bank (IBRD), and the Bank for International Settlements (BIS) were formally established; these organizations established the post-war international financial order.[9] What is worth considering is: Why has the result of the 44-nation wrestling in the Bretton Woods Conference dominated the international financial system for more than 70 years, with its impact still felt today?

The third case is the US dollar internationalization system established by the Marshall Plan. This program, led by the USA, was launched in April 1948 and terminated in 1951. During this period, European countries established the Organization for Economic Cooperation and Development to match the Marshall Plan and created a counterpart fund to solve the problem of currency conversion. USA aid to Europe included funds, technology, personnel, and other aspects. Among them, financial aid flowed like this: the USA provided US dollars to European countries, while European countries used US dollars as foreign exchange to purchase US goods; apart from Germany, European countries basically did not repay the aid funds; apart from Germany, who used the aid funds for private enterprises reinvestment, most European countries used the funds to fill their fiscal deficit. In this system, the US dollars stagnated in Europe and formed the "Eurodollar." Thus, the global currency system gradually developed from the "gold and silver bimetallism" to the "gold standard," then to the "gold to US dollar and US dollar to other currencies" (fixed exchange rate: 35 US dollars to 1 oz of gold), and then to the "fixed exchange rate system of US dollar to other currencies" (gold and US dollar decoupled on August 15, 1971), and finally to the "floating exchange rate system of US dollar to other currencies" (established in 1976 by the Jamaica Agreement), and eventually, formed a strong US dollar internationalization system.[10]

All the above case studies illustrate financial thoughts, financial strategies, financial policies, financial systems, and financial behavior promoted by the liberal economy-pursuing US government on a national level. During the competition and development of contemporary world economies, the most effective measure taken by the US government against other countries is "financial sanctions." As can be seen, the top-level financial arrangement of developed nations has already commenced. As far as developing countries are concerned, economic exchanges often develop from merchandise trade to general service trade, and then to high-end service trade; economic openness is often promoted from current account to capital account; even the economic free trade zones that many nations have tried to establish develop from trade facilitation to investment and financing facilitation, and then to capital account convertibility. This gap reminds us that it is imperative for regional governments to participate in economic competition and for the nation to participate in financial arrangement and carry out top-level financial design.

Notes

1. Chen Yunxian. *Foresighted Leading*. Beijing: Peking University Press, 2011, pp. 15–32.
2. Chen Yunxian and Qiu Jianwei. *Government Foresighted Leading: Theory and Practice of the World's Regional Economic Development*. Beijing: Peking University Press, 2013, pp. 114–116.
3. IMI is an industry–university–research partnership, which was set up under the support of the American federal government or state governments. Each

IMI focuses on a certain area, combining public and private resources to create a more vigorous national innovative ecosystem. The aim is to accelerate the transformation of innovations into products and the development of medium-sized and small enterprises.

4. Chen Yunxian. *Foresighted Leading*. Beijing: Peking University Press, 2011, pp. 128–131; "Pearl River Delta, Waving Goodbye to Outmoded Towns, Outmoded Factory Buildings, Outmoded Villages", *People's Daily*, May 23, 2016.
5. Chen Yunxian. *Foresighted Leading*. Beijing: Peking University Press, 2011, pp. 47–56.
6. *Report on the Work of the Guangdong Provincial Government*, January 25, 2016.
7. Comparison between developed and underdeveloped regions: In the financial revenue structure, generally speaking, underdeveloped regions' non-tax revenue accounts for a large proportion, and is not stable, while land sale revenue and government debt are high, therefore there is a high chance of acute financial risk. In the financial expenditure structure, generally speaking, underdeveloped regions' expense on economic development accounts for a large proportion, while that on social welfare accounts for a relatively small proportion. With developed regions, the opposite is the case.
8. Henry Cabot Lodge, ed. *The Works of Alexander Hamilton*, Vol. 9. New York: G. P. Putnam's Sons, 1971, p. 224.
9. Eric Rauchway. *The Money Makers: How Roosevelt and Keynes Ended the Depression, Defeated Fascism, and Secured a Prosperous Peace*. New York: Basic Books, 2015, pp. 183–202.
10. Shao Huaming and Hou Chen. "Internationalization of RMB: Status Quo and Path Choice—Taking the Internationalization of USD as an Example", *Finance & Economics*, No. 11 (2015): 23–33.

Chapter 5
Regional Government Competition

1 The Broad and Narrow Senses of Government Competition

The concept of "region" is a relative one. Globally, a country is a region. Nationally, a city is a region. Not only do similarities exist between regions, so do differences. Regional government usually refers to the governmental organization that manages the administrative affairs of the region, which has a relatively stable region under the jurisdiction, relatively concentrated population and regional governance institutions. Regional government is public and mandatory.

Regional competitiveness refers to the force that can support the sustainable survival and development of a region, i.e., during the process of competition and development of a region, compared with other regions, the ability to attract, compete for, possess, regulate, and transform resources, as well as the ability to compete for, possess, and regulate the market, namely the ability to optimize the allocation of resources required for its own development. Put simply, it is the ability to attract resources and compete for the market that a region needs for its own development. With the methodology of comparative economics, an index system can be established to analyze and evaluate regional competitiveness, so as to find problems during regional development and factors to enhance competition. Therein lies the positive significance that through studying the ways to enhance regional competitiveness, we would create competitive advantages and optimize the allocation of resources to promote the scientific and sustainable development of the regional economy.

Regional resources or urban resources, defined from the perspective of economics, and as discussed in Chap. 3 "Scarcity and Generation of Resources," have broad and narrow definitions. Broadly speaking, urban resources include industrial resources, livelihood resources, and infrastructure resources; narrowly speaking, urban resources refer to urban infrastructure resources, including the investment and construction of hardware and software infrastructure, as well as the investment, development, and operation of modern intelligent cities. Henceforth, the regional economy

Y. Chen, *New Economic Engine: Effective Government and Efficient Market*, China Academic Library, https://doi.org/10.1007/978-981-15-2922-1_5

or urban economy in its broad sense includes industrial economy, livelihood economy, and the economy based mainly on infrastructure construction; whereas the regional economy or urban economy in its narrow sense specifically refers to the investment and development of infrastructure. Consequently, it follows that regional government competition differs in its broad sense and its narrow sense.

Broadly speaking, regional government competition includes the competitions in operational resources (industrial economy), non-operational resources (livelihood economy), and quasi-operational resources (urban economy). Narrowly speaking, regional government competition refers to competition for the investment and construction of quasi-operational resources (infrastructure resources). As far as nations are concerned, their three major tasks are maintaining stability, promoting development, and handling emergencies. As far as regional governments are concerned, promoting economic growth, implementing urban construction, and protecting social livelihood are their three major economic functions. Regional governments perform these three functions, classify various types of tangible and intangible resources that the regions already have or would potentially have based on economics, allocate resources, make policy measures, and analyze and compare the competition among regional governments. In essence, these measures are to discover, create, and raise the competitiveness of the regions.

Regional government competition can mainly be divided into three categories.

The first category, competition in livelihood economy, mainly relates to the resources that are associated with the people's livelihood, known in market economy as non-operational resources. These are mainly social public goods resources, including economy (guarantee), history, geography, image, spirit, value, emergency, security, relief, and other social needs of the region. The principles of governments' policies accordingly should be "social guarantee, general underpinning, fairness and justice, effective promotion." The perfection of such policies and measures serves to maintain social coordination and stability, enhance and optimize the environment for the investment and development of the regional economy.

The second category, competition in the industrial economy, mainly relates to the resources that are associated with economic growth, known in the market economy as operational resources. These are mainly industrial resources, including the primary, secondary, and tertiary industries. Due to differences in economic geographical and natural conditions, the pace of development of the primary, secondary, and tertiary industries, as well as their focuses, varies in different nations. Nevertheless, many nations have meticulously developed their primary industries, optimized the development of their secondary industries, and accelerated the development of their tertiary industries, and continually succeeded. The principles of governments' policies accordingly should be "planning, guidance; support, coordination; supervision, management." The perfection of such policies and measures serves to promote market openness, fairness, and justice, to effectively promote the coordinated development of the industrial economy, and to increase the overall productivity of the society.

The third category, competition in the urban economy, mainly relates to the resources that are associated with urban construction, known in the market economy as quasi-operational resources. These are mainly urban resources, including the public service system, which is used to ensure that normal social and economic activities of the nation or region can be carried out; and the software and hardware infrastructure, which is used to provide public services for production and life, such as services in transportation, post and telecommunications, power and water supply, landscaping, environmental protection, education, science and technology, culture, health, sports, press and publication, radio, film, television, and even services for the development and construction of modern intelligent cities. The reasons why they are quasi-operational resources are that their development and management can be carried out by the government in the form of providing public goods—in this regard, they are non-operational resources, being public welfare and livelihood economy in nature, or can also be promoted by the government and enterprises with the assistance of the market—in this regard, they are operational resources, being commodities and industrial economy in nature. In the latter case, urban resources are developed, operated, and managed by the government or enterprises in the market environment. The operation depends not only on the financial status of the government, but also on the market demand and the public acceptability. Government practice across the world, including the successful experience of China's reform and opening up, has told us that in order to prevent the urban resources from lying idle and being wasted, or the low-quality and disorderly management of urban construction, regional governments across the world will develop, operate, and manage part or even most of the quasi-operational resources, that is, the investment and development projects of infrastructure under the context of market. At this point, its carrier, that is, the equity nature and structure of infrastructure construction projects, must conform to market competition rules; its operation, that is, the investment, operation, and management of infrastructure construction projects must be realized through market competition. Henceforth, by participating in the allocation and competition of quasi-operational resources, that is, the urban economy, the government promotes the comprehensive and sustainable development of urban construction and social economy.

The three types of competition above, that is, the optimal allocation of resources and supporting policies, constitute a big system, and governments compete substantially with one another in a big market system. Consequently, regional governments across the world compete with one another on the effectiveness of their allocation of the three types of resources above and the completeness of their supporting policies and measures, thereby promoting economic growth and development. Competition between regional governments across the world is manifested not only broadly in the three types of economy mentioned above and their supporting policies and measures, but also narrowly in the third type, that is, the investment and construction of the software and hardware urban infrastructure, and even in the development and construction projects of modern intelligent cities, and their supporting policies and measures. This book discusses regional government competition in various chapters, which generally refers to competition in the broad sense, but focuses more on competition in the narrow sense.

2 The Connections and Differences Between Government Competition and Enterprise Competition

The competition between enterprises is reflected predominantly in the competition for industrial resource allocation in industrial economy. The competition between regional governments is reflected predominantly in the competition for urban resource allocation in the urban economy. The two systems are relatively independent, complementing each other. Their connections and differences are as follows:

(1) On areas of competition: Enterprises are subjects in microeconomics. Enterprise competition occurs mainly in the commodity market, mainly in the allocation of industrial resources in the industrial economy. With manufacturers as the subjects, market equilibrium theory is the dominant theory in traditional classical economics. On the premise of maximizing profits, supply, demand, market equilibrium price, perfect competitive market, monopolistic competitive market, oligopolistic market, and the different competitive strategies in different market structures are the main factors affecting competition among enterprises. Enterprise competition sets the premise and foundation for regional government competition. On the other hand, the regional government is the research subject in mezzoeconomics. Competition between regional governments occurs mainly in the factor market, mainly in the allocation of urban resources in the urban economy. Factor markets include land, capital, talents, property rights, technology and information, and other hardware and software markets. Regional governments need not only to grasp the quantity, quality, structure, and distribution of the urban resource factors, but also to formulate policies and systems to coordinate the allocation of urban resource factors in the region and attract foreign resource factors, thereby optimizing the allocation of resources and increasing regional competitiveness. The competition in the factor market affects the competition of enterprises in the commodity market.

(2) On means of competition: The main means by which enterprises maximize profits are improving labor productivity to effectively influence costs, prices, supply and demand, scale, and optimizing the allocation of industrial resources to minimize costs. On the other hand, regional governments attempt to improve total factor productivity to promote sustainable economic growth for the region. For the regional government, after the simple expansion of tangible factors such as land, projects, and capital, the bottleneck of diminishing marginal return on capital makes the "extensive" economic growth unsustainable. When the input of all the tangible factors in the region remains unchanged, regional governments can still inject new driving energy into regional economic development and urban construction by promoting technological innovation, optimizing resource allocation, restructuring, and improving intangible factors such as institution, organization, law, and the environment.

(3) On the path of competition: Enterprise performance is mainly led by input-oriented growth, whose continuous improvement results from the continuous

input of production factors by enterprises, such as capital, labor, land, technology, entrepreneurship, and others. The strategy of input is initially quantitative expansion, gradually developing to the stage of quality improvement, and then to the stage of expansionary management, where sustainable and effective input become the key. Regional government performance is mainly led by efficiency-oriented growth. As seen from the development practice of regional governments across the globe, their regional economic growth paths evolve from a "factor-driven stage" (also known as "resource allocation stage"), to an "investment-driven stage" (also known as "efficiency enhancement stage"), and to an "innovation-driven stage" (also known as "sustainable growth stage"). Regional governments promote efficiency-oriented economic growth by optimizing the combination of resource factors.

(4) On competition orientation: Enterprises are guided by expanding demand. Enterprise competition needs to be based on market demand; from quantity and structure of demand to enterprise strategies, whether they can meet market demand or not become the key to determine the success or failure of enterprises. Regional governments are guided by optimizing supply. Effective allocation of the supply of tangible resource factors such as land, capital, projects, technology, and talents, effective coordination of the supply of intangible resource factors such as planning, investment, consumption, price, taxation, interest rate, exchange rate and law, and the promotion of supply-side structural reform through innovation in values, institutions, organizations, and technology are the definitive direction for regional governments to develop economy, construct cities, and improve livelihood.

(5) On competition mode: Enterprises use the Enterprise Resource Planning (ERP) system to effectively integrate the management of their resources of materials, capital, information, and customers, to assist enterprises to achieve effective cross-regional, cross-sectoral, and cross-industrial coordination and allocation in the flow of materials, people, money, and information, so as to integrate resources effectively, adjust functions expeditiously and improve productivity, with market as its orientation, and ultimately effectively improve the competitiveness of enterprises. On the other hand, through the District Resource Planning (DRP) system, regional governments can effectively allocate various resource factors within their regions, such as land, population, finance, environment, technologies, and policies, to assist regional governments' layout around regional planning and development strategies using systematic management ideas and means. They can allocate regional resources and enhance regional competitiveness based on the judgment of market changes, thereby fulfilling the optimization of regional total factor productivity, and even the sustainable regional socioeconomic development.

3 The Forms of Regional Government Competition

As can be seen from above, enterprise competition is the competition in industrial resource allocation in the industrial economy, that is, competition in the commodity market, whereas regional government competition is the competition in urban resource allocation in the urban economy, that is, competition in the factor market, dominated mainly by the software and hardware infrastructure. Competitions between enterprises and between regional governments are the two levels of competition systems in the modern market economy; they are mutually independent and interrelated and together constitute the dual competitors in the modern market economy. Firstly, competition at the enterprise level is the basis of all competition in the market economy. Enterprise competition motivates competition among regional governments. Regional government competition is mainly in optimizing resource allocation of institutions, policies, projects, and the environment, etc. It is another kind of competition on top of enterprise competition, which in turn influences, supports, and promotes enterprise competition. Secondly, enterprise competition system exists only among enterprises. Governments at any level can only play the roles of planner and guide in industrial economy/industrial resource allocation, supporter and coordinator in commodity production, and supervisor and manager of the market order and have no rights to directly intervene in the micro-affairs of enterprises. The competition system of regional government exists only among regional governments, which should adhere to the laws of the market economy, and compete in projects, policies, and specific affairs in the allocation of urban resources, economic development, urban construction, and social livelihood. Regional government competition in the narrow sense is the main driving and leading force behind regional government competition in the broad sense.

The specific forms of regional government competition are as follows:

(1) Competition in projects, of which there are three main types: firstly, major national projects, including key national projects, national science, and technology support programs, key national technology infrastructure construction plans, major engineering projects, and industrialization projects financed by the state; secondly, social investment projects, such as high-tech industries, emerging industries, equipment manufacturing industries, raw materials industries, and financial, logistics, and other services; thirdly, projects with the introduction of foreign capital, such as intelligent manufacturing, cloud computing, big data, the Internet of Things, construction of intelligent cities, and others. During the process of implementing various projects, regional governments can firstly, directly introduce funds, talents, and industries; secondly, effectively solve the problems of financing and land expropriation in the region by virtue of the legitimacy of project policies and the rationality of public services; and thirdly, through practical implementation of projects, guide the development of regional land, construct urban facilities, attract more investment, promote industrial development, optimize resource allocation, and enhance policy capacity, and ultimately, promote sustainable regional socioeconomic development.

Hence, project competition has become the focus of competition and direction of development for regional governments across the world. Project awareness, development awareness, efficiency awareness, advantage awareness, condition awareness, policy awareness, and risk awareness have become the necessary requirements for regional governments across the world to participate in competition with market economy.

(2) Competition in the supporting industrial chain: In general, each region has its own industrial base and characteristics, depending mostly on the natural resource endowments of the region. How to maintain and optimize the resource endowments of the region, and how to gather high-end resources from outside the region? The key is the optimization of the industrial structure and effective allocation of the industrial chain; and the breakthrough lies in high-end development of the industries, formation of industrial agglomeration, and leading industrial clusters. The competition of the regional government's supporting industrial chain lies mainly in two aspects: first, the factors of production. Low-end or primary factors of production cannot form stable and sustainable competitiveness; only by introducing and investing in high-end factors of production, such as industrial technology, modern information technology, network resources, transportation facilities, professionals, research, and development think tanks, etc., can strong industries with competitive advantages be established. Second, the industrial clusters and supporting industries. The theory on regional competitiveness suggests that the effective establishment of supporting industries led by existing industrial base within the region can reduce the transaction costs of enterprises and increase their profitability. The industrial smile curve suggests that most values are concentrated at the two ends of the industrial value chain, namely research and development, and the market. An important path to sustainable regional development is to cultivate superior industries, complete the industrial chain, and attract investment in accordance with the industrial structure.

(3) Competition in talents, science, and technology: In this field of competition, the most fundamental is to establish the notion that talent resources are the primary resources, and science and technology are the primary productive forces; the most basic is to improve the local talent training system and increase the investment in local talent training and in science and technology innovation; the most critical is to create conditions to attract, bring in, cultivate, and utilize talents. The main indicators to measure the competitiveness of scientific and technological talents include regional scientific and technological talent resource index, the number of people engaged in scientific and technological activities per 10,000 people, the number of scientists and engineers per 10,000 people, the number of students enrolled in higher education per 10,000 people, the index of annual input of scientific and technological talents per 10,000 people, the total operating expenditure on scientific and technological activities, the proportion of expenditure on science and technology in GDP, per capita scientific research funds, the percentage of scientific and technological appropriations in local financial expenditure, per capita financial expenditure on education, the total amount of

local financial expenditure on education, and the number of full-time teachers employed in higher education, among others. Through diligently improving the relevant indicators, regional governments elevate the competitiveness of local talents and science and technology.

(4) Competition in treasury and finance: Regional fiscal competition includes competition in fiscal revenue and fiscal expenditure. The main route of fiscal revenue increase is to promote economic growth and raise tax revenue. Fiscal expenditure includes social consumption expenditure, transfer expenditure, and investment expenditure, with its main competition occurring in the area of investment expenditure, including government's investment in infrastructure, research and development of science and technology, policy-based financing (supporting industries in urgent need of development), and others. Fiscal investment expenditure is an important driving force of economic growth. Under the circumstances of limited financial revenue and expenditure, regional governments across the world actively build various platforms for investment and financing, mobilize, and attract financial resources such as capital, talents, and information from regional, domestic, and international financial institutions, to serve regional economic development, urban construction, and social livelihood. Regional governments also compete with one another for various preferential policies, such as the emphasis of fiscal expenditure, financial measures to absorb capital, etc.

(5) Competition in infrastructure: As mentioned above, the competition in this field includes the construction of the software and hardware urban infrastructure, as well as the development and operation of modern intelligent cities. Infrastructure hardware includes expressways, railways, ports, aviation, and other transport facilities; electricity, natural gas, and other energy facilities; optical cable, network, and other information platform facilities; and science and technology parks, industrial parks, business incubation parks, creative industry parks, and other engineering infrastructure. Infrastructure software includes education, science and technology, health care, sports, culture, social welfare, and other public infrastructure. Intelligent city development includes big data, cloud computing, the Internet of Things, and other intelligent technology platforms. The infrastructure system of a region supports its socioeconomic development and predominantly includes three types, namely advanced, adaptive, and lagging. If the supply of regional infrastructure is moderately advanced, not only will it directly strengthen regional competitiveness, but also create high-quality urban structure, size of facilities, and spatial layout, prompt enterprises in market competition to reduce costs and improve productivity, thereby promoting industrial development. The degree of completeness of regional infrastructure will directly affect the current and future state of regional economic development.

(6) Competition in the environment system: Environment here mainly refers to the ecological environment, humanistic environment, policy environment, and social credit system. Developing investment should be in harmony with protecting the ecosystem; attracting investment should be coupled with policy services;

pursuing wealth should be balanced with repaying the society; legal supervision and social credit should support each other. These are the indispensable development environments for regional government competition. The building of a good environmental system has become the secret of success for regional governments to attract investment, develop projects, and promote continuous economic development, as proven by the experience of successful regions both at home and abroad.

(7) Competition in import and export: In an open international economic system, regional import and export competition across the world has become an important link influencing regional competitiveness. It is mainly manifested in four aspects. Firstly, in the development of processing trade and general trade, regional governments across the world endeavor to reduce the proportion of processing trade and increase that of general trade, in order to enhance the motivation for regional trade in goods and services. Secondly, in foreign investment, regional governments across the world attempt to push for the overseas distribution of enterprises and compete for overseas projects in order to promote the distribution of their regional interests and extend their market chains overseas. Thirdly, in terms of capital export, regional governments across the world try to promote capital account convertibility; in other words, under the circumstances of facilitating international current account investment, take various measures to promote the circulation of money capital and facilitate free currency exchange. Fourthly, in terms of import, especially the introduction of high-tech products, industries, and projects, regional governments across the world shall fully take preferential policy measures to attract, support, and even spare no expense to assist their investment, distribution, and production. The result of import and export competition is one of the important factors affecting regional economic growth across the world.

(8) Competition in policy systems: This can be divided into two levels: Firstly, regional governments' foreign policy system, and secondly, the series of regional governments' domestic policies. It also holds true between nations. As policies themselves are public goods, characterized by non-exclusiveness and can be easily imitated, thus, a good competitive policy system must contain the following characteristics. Firstly, it is practical, that is, it is realistic and satisfies the requirements of economic and social development. Secondly, it is advanced, that is, it has predictability and is leading and innovative. Thirdly, it is operational, that is, policies are clear, pertinent, and implementable. Fourthly, it is organizational, that is, there are specialized agencies and personnel responsible for its implementation. Finally, it is result-oriented, that is, it has mechanisms for its inspection, supervision, assessment, and evaluation, including exerting a third-party influence to effectively realize policy objectives. The level of completeness of regional policy systems across the world has a great impact on regional competitiveness.

(9) Competition in management efficiency: The management efficiency of regional government is the overall reflection of its administrative management activities, pace, quality, and efficiency. It includes four categories, namely macro-efficiency, micro-efficiency, organizational efficiency, and personal efficiency. As far as administrative compliance is concerned, regional governments should meet the standards of legitimacy, interests, and quality in the competition of management efficiency; as far as administrative efficiency is concerned, regional governments should meet the standards of quantity, time, pace, and budget. The competition in the management efficiency of regional governments is essentially the competition in their organizational system, principal responsibilities, service consciousness, work skills, and technology platforms. Developed regional governments have already in practice pioneered the competition of management efficiency by engaging parallel and integrated modes of service.

Regional government competition is mainly manifested in the nine areas of specific competition as described above and is essentially to solve the following problems during the process of allocating urban resources: What policies on operational resources (industrial economy) should be adopted to invigorate the enterprises? What policies on non-operational resources (livelihood economy) should be adopted to create a sound environment? On quasi-operational resources (urban economy) what forms of participation to take, what rules and regulations to abide by, and what policies to be made to fulfill sustainable regional growth? Therefore, the essence of regional government competition is the competition in the effective allocation of the three categories of resources. Its emphasis lies with the allocation of quasi-operational resources, that is, the competition in narrowly defined urban economy with infrastructure investment and construction as its main entity.

4 "Voting by Foot" to Select Regional Governments

Scale effects, cluster effects, and neighborhood effects of urban economic development can be formed by regional government competition.

The scale effects of urban economy refer to the effects of "1 + 1 > 2" produced by the organic combination of various factors of production after the total economic volume of the region has reached a certain scale and level. That is, the growth in the scale of the urban economy brings about the elevation of economic benefits and comprehensive social benefits. Speaking from the level of the regional government, the factors determining the scale of regional economy lie mainly in the policy arrangements and supporting measures on the development and usage of the three types of urban resources. In other words, what policies should be adopted to plan, guide, coordinate, support, supervise, and manage the operational resources (industrial economy) to invigorate the enterprises? What policies on non-operational resources (livelihood economy) should be adopted to attain fairness, justice, guarantee, and promotion, to optimize the investment environment? What policies on quasi-operational resources (urban economy) should be adopted to promote sustainable development? The specific forms as described in the previous section on the nine aspects ultimately determine the scale effects of the region. That is to say, regional government competition determines the scale effect of the urban infrastructure, the scale effect of population and the scale effect it brings to entrepreneurship and employment, the scale effect of science and technology, the scale effect of capital, the scale effect of industry, the scale effect of the degree of market openness and trade, as well as the effects of policies and organizational management, and others. Regional government competition can form and strengthen the positive scale effects of the urban economy.

The cluster effects of urban economy refer to the economic effect and comprehensive social effect produced by the spatial concentration of various economic resources and activities in the region, as well as the centripetal force resulting from that concentration, which makes various economic resources and activities congregate in this region. It is the basic factor for the continual expansion and development of urban economy. The cluster effects of the urban economy include the cluster effects of economy, culture, talents, science and technology, capital, transportation infrastructure, organization management, policy measures, and others. For example, the cluster effects of industries include firstly, the formation of vertical industrial clusters to promote scientific and technological innovation; secondly, the extension of industrial chains to form a virtuous cycle of "resources → products → wastes → resources → products," and their comprehensive use; thirdly, the attainment of energy conservation and emission reduction, ecological and environmental protection, as well as the organic combination of economic benefits and comprehensive social benefits. The cluster effects of industries bring cost advantages and promote the division of labor and cooperation. Enterprises in the region share the advantages of industrial brands, thus, the scale of enterprise investment can continue to expand, the level of strategic management can continue to improve, and the social service system can improve day by day. The development of industrial clusters further promotes the transformation of regional economic growth mode. The advantageous cluster of talents, land, capital, technology, management, services, and others forms radiation effects, accelerates the process of industrialization, urbanization, and informatization, pushes for the effective utilization of various resources in the region, and promotes the sustainable development of the economy. To enhance the cluster effects of the urban economy, regional governments should take the initiatives in the nine major forms of competitions.

The neighborhood effects of the urban economy mean the characteristics of the regional environment can influence the mentality and choice of the behavior of people. When people are generally expecting to build a harmonious, comfortable, and convenient environment, striving to attain the greatest rewards at the lowest cost in economic activities, the influence of the regional environment will promote the transmission and exchange of the mood and economic behavior. That is what we call the neighborhood effects. Needless to say, neighborhood effects can be beneficial or detrimental, benign or malignant, positive or negative. The regional environment and comprehensive social development level will also directly affect the neighborhood effects, which include regional economy, culture, talents, science and technology, capital, transportation infrastructure, and the organizational efficiency and policy effectiveness of regional governments. Regional government competition is objectively conducive to guiding beneficial, positive, and benign neighborhood effects into play.

Due to the existence of regional government competition, in an open social and economic system, there arises investors' choice of where their factors of production should flow, that is, the problems of "voting by foot."[1] Investors' choices in the flow of people, money, and materials will prompt regional governments to provide a better public environment and public services. "Voting by foot" is to choose cities and regions, which in essence is to choose regional governments, regional environment, regional services, and others. Regional governments' planning, guidance, support, coordination, supervision and management of the industrial economy, safeguard of the fairness and justice of livelihood economy and its effective promotion, investment and construction of the software and hardware urban infrastructure and intelligent cities, as well as the nine aspects of regional competition in the three types of economy described earlier can effectively enhance the attractiveness of the regional brands.

Note

1. Charles M. Tiebout. "A Pure Theory of Local Expenditures", *The Journal of Political Economy*, Vol. 64, No. 5 (1956): 416–424.

Chapter 6
Modern Market Economy

1 The Horizontal System of Modern Market

After the systematic analyses earlier, the purpose of this chapter is to further clarify that in the horizontal market system, not only are there market subjects in industrial economy—enterprises, there are also market subjects in urban economy—regional governments, as well as market subjects in international economy who provide quasi-operational resources, that is, public goods, including market subjects responsible for the development of space resources in space economy and marine resources in marine economy—governments or enterprises. So to speak, firstly, the market exists not only in industrial economy, but also in other economic forms. Secondly, in the horizontal market system (including industrial economy, urban economy, and international economy such as space economy, marine economy, and others), there are dual competitors—enterprises and governments. And finally, industrial economy is the fundamental field of market economy, whereas urban economy and international economy (including space, deep-sea and other resources that develop through the times) are generative fields of market economy; they are mutually independent and yet, interrelated, and belong to the competition systems of different levels in modern market economy. The multi-level market competition systems collectively constitute modern market economy.

Traditional market theory, also known as firm equilibrium theory, specifically studies how firms determine the price and output of their products in different types of markets. As a result, four basic market types can be distinguished: perfectly competitive market, monopolistic competitive market, oligopolistic market and perfectly monopolistic market. Hence, traditional market theory analyses the market, firms and industries; cost, income and output; and even firm equilibrium in the perfectly competitive market, perfectly monopolistic market, monopolistic competitive market and oligopolistic market. As was known from earlier discussions, firstly, traditional market theory focuses mainly on industrial economy, or rather, the theory itself is clarified in industrial economy. Secondly, Adam Smith's *Wealth of Nations*, being the

Y. Chen, *New Economic Engine: Effective Government and Efficient Market*, China Academic Library, https://doi.org/10.1007/978-981-15-2922-1_6

pioneering work of economics and market economy theory, is undoubtedly a great work. However, limited by the times, after criticizing mercantilism and physiocracy, Adam Smith mainly based on industrial economy to investigate commodity, price, supply and demand, competition and market, and failed to discuss the economic operations of new generative resources and fields in new generative economics. Thirdly, in order to deal with the massive unemployment of British workers in the 1920s and the Great Depression of the United States and even the world economy in the early 1930s, Keynes attempted to lever a new field, urban economy, that is, the investment and construction of infrastructure, to stimulate effective demand. However, confined by the market theory in industrial economy, he failed to explain the effects of governments in their participation and intervention in the investment and construction of urban infrastructure. Finally, as discussed earlier, the contradiction between practice and theory as reflected by market failure or government failure, in essence, is not a problem of the market, but a problem of traditional market theory; not a problem of the imperfection of market theory rooted in industrial economy, but a self-contradictory situation that results inevitably from confining to this theory to define, explain and analyze the economic operation in the field of new generative resources.

Urban economic theory, in the narrow sense, mainly investigates why the government, as provider of public goods, and maintainer of market rules, becomes a participant in the investment and a competitor in the projects during the process of investment, construction, operation and management of the software and hardware urban infrastructure, and even intelligent cities; as infrastructure, why some of the public goods become operational projects in the market system and promote the development of the regional economy. In this theory, urban economy possesses market entities, projects, prices and supply-demand relations different from industrial economy. In addition, being an important field in the horizontal market system, the urban economy formed by generative resources is playing increasingly important roles both in practice and in theory.

There are also topics on the development of international economic resources (such as deep-sea economic resources, space economic resources), which are also generative resources. On the one hand, these new generative resources expand the scope of the market to be explored and their allocation needs to be optimized; on the other hand, we need to enrich market theory and improve market rules in accordance with these new situations. There have been constant media reports recently that it is an opportune time now to conduct "aerospace" as a big business.[1] Reportedly, China Rocket shall develop commercial launch services, sub-orbital flight experience and space resource utilization. For example, on commercial launch services, the company will provide space satellite networks, space lifts, space shuttles, space special vehicles and others. On sub-orbital flights, the company will provide various products and services such as ground weightless simulation, 360° VR experience, sub-orbital space travel and others in accordance with the ages, physical conditions and interests of tourists. Backed by the powerful Chinese aerospace industry, with the US space exploration technology company (Space X) as its benchmark, China Rocket plans to gradually inject assets, introduce strategic investors, and promote the advent of commercialization era of Chinese rockets. Major powers have already begun competing in this field where returns on investment have always been high. Under these circumstances, how should "aerospace economics" be conceived? How should it develop? How effective is it? Aerospace economy faces this problem, and even more so for space economy in a broader sense. These new circumstances are constantly broadening the fields of the market on the one hand, and on the other, calling for the interpretation of the investors and rules of the game that are different from those in industrial economy.

2 The Vertical System of Modern Market

The traditional market system can be looked at mainly from four levels. Firstly, in terms of entities in circulation, the traditional market is composed of the commodity market and the factors of production market; secondly, in terms of spatial scope, it is composed of different regional markets at all levels of various scopes; thirdly, in terms of institutional settings, it is composed of various market organizations and market intermediary organizations; and lastly, in terms of specific methods, it consists of the spot market, forward market and future market.

In contrast, the modern market system emphasizes the systematicity of market structure, especially the systematicity of functional structure. The market functional structure is firstly the interests adjustment system, secondly the competition system, and thirdly the information dissemination system. Therefore, the vertical system of modern market should include at least the following six aspects:

(1) The market factor system: It is composed of various types of markets (including the commodity market, factors market and financial market, etc.), and the most basic elements in various types of markets, namely price, supply and demand, competition, and others.
(2) The market organization system: It is the concentration of the main entities or organizers of market factors and market activities, including various types of market entities (such as the retail market, wholesale market, talent market, labor market, financial market, and others), various market intermediaries (including consultation, training, information, accounting, law, property rights, asset valuation and other service agencies), and market management organizations (such as various chambers of commerce and industry associations).
(3) The market legal system: Market economy has the characteristics of property rights economy, contract economy and normative economy. Therefore, the system of laws and regulations regulating market value orientation, transaction behavior, contract behavior and property rights behavior as a whole constitutes the market legal system. It includes market-related legislation, law enforcement, justice, legal education, etc.
(4) The market supervision system: It is a system of policies implementation based on the market legal system, which meets the needs of the market economy,

including the supervision and management of institutions, businesses, markets, implementation of policies and regulations, and others.

(5) The market environment system: It mainly includes the three aspects of foundation of real economy, corporate governance structure and social credit system. What is important to this system is to establish and improve the market credit system, regulate trust relations, credit instruments, credit intermediaries and other relevant credit elements by law, and establish the social credit governance mechanism, with the improvement of the market credit guarantee mechanism as a starting point.

(6) The market infrastructure: It is a complete market facility system including various hardware and software. Among them, market service networks, supporting facilities and technologies, various market payment and settlement systems, science and technology information systems and others, are the infrastructure necessary for a mature market economy.

The vertical system of modern market and its six subsystems have the following characteristics:

(1) The formation of the vertical system of modern market is a gradual historical process. During the early development of market economy, the US mainstream accepted the laissez-faire economic concept, the market factor and market organization systems were developed and promoted, and objection against government intervention in the economy prevailed. In 1890, the United States Congress promulgated the Sherman Antitrust Act, the first anti-monopoly law in American history, prohibiting monopolistic agreements and monopolistic behavior. In 1914, the United States promulgated the Federal Trade Commission Act and the Clayton Antitrust Act to supplement and improve the Sherman Act. Since then, the anti-monopoly system and regulatory practice in the United States have undergone nearly a hundred years of evolution and improvement, and the whole market has formed a pattern of dynamic coexistence of monopoly and competition, development and regulation. Since the 1990s, the information communication and network technology in the United States have developed explosively, the capacity to drive market innovation, and infrastructure upgrades have become the main manifestations of market competition. At the same time, the anti-monopoly objectives of the US government are no longer restricted to simple prevention of market monopoly and price manipulation; technology monopoly that is not for patent protection and network oligopoly are also part of them. During this period, the market environment system and market infrastructure of the United States have been further improved and developed through the improvements of infrastructure like market registration, settlement, trusteeship and backup, improvements in the abilities to handle major disasters and technical failures, enhancements in market information system, improvements in the construction of the credit system, sharing of market supervision data, etc. All these have pushed the market system to a modern stage, and market competition has leaped into a stage promoted by total factors and systematic participation.

(2) The six aspects of the vertical system of modern market are unified. On the one hand, the six market subsystems are interconnected and interactive, organically integrated into a mature market economy system. During the operation of the market economy in practice, any missing subsystem will lead to market deficiencies in that area, causing economic losses to the nation. During the development of market economy across the world, such typical cases are common throughout. On the other hand, within the six market subsystems, factors are also interconnected, interactive and organically unified with each other. For example, in the market factor system, apart from the interconnections of various commodity markets, factor markets and financial markets, in the factor markets, the standardization and development of land markets, gradual establishment of a unified urban and rural labor market, active development of the technology markets, vigorous enhancement of property rights (including technological property rights) trading markets, etc. are all important measures to mutually improve and collectively perfect a modern market system.

(3) The six aspects of the vertical system of modern market are orderly; only an orderly market system is efficient. For example, in an orderly pricing mechanism of commodities, factors and projects, during the formation of the investment price of commodities, factors and projects (resources or generative resources), the market should fully demonstrate its basic role in resource allocation, and set prices according to the supply-demand relationship, and the status of the scarcity of resources and resource generation reflected in the market, thereby promoting the orderly operation of the modern market system. The orderly competition mechanism of commodities, factors and projects is another example. Competition is an inevitable product of market economy, and also a prerequisite of realizing market economy. Only through competition can the prices of commodities, factors and projects fluctuate in the market, and resources be allocated to the most efficient enterprises, regions or phases, thereby realizing the survival of the fittest market entities. Market segmentation, blockade and monopoly are all barriers that must be removed from the modern market system. The orderly opening mechanism of commodities, factors and projects is a further example. In the open modern market system, commodities, factors and projects are open to investors from different regions, industries, home and abroad, all of whom can enter out of own's accord, choose supply and demand at free will, and invest and develop independently. However, this kind of opening must be gradual, safe, stable and orderly. This shows once again that the six aspects of the vertical system of modern market are mutually independent and yet mutually restrictive; as an example, competition and supervision of the market, freedom and the rule of law, etc., are complete systems of unity of opposites.

(4) The functions of the six aspects of the vertical modern market system are fragile. The reasons are as follows. Firstly, incomplete understanding: As the market subjects (namely, participants in the commodity market, factor market and project market) have their own demands for interests, during the operation of the market in practice, they tend to focus only on freedom, competition and demand, instead of the rule of law, supervision and balances, resulting in biases

in the functions of the six aspects of the vertical system of modern market. Secondly, the untimeliness of policies: Various investors are the main participants of the market, while regional governments across the world are the main supervisors of the market. However, over the historical interactions of the unity of opposites between the government and market, due to the influence of traditional market economy theory, the government is usually inactive, lagging, or when faced with world economic crisis, makes up by "patching and filling holes", rendering the six aspects of the vertical system of modern market unable to fully function. Thirdly, the impact of economic globalization: In the global market system where there is imperfection in legislation, joint law enforcement and coordinated supervision measures, there exist many problems such as vacuum in regulations, regulatory arbitrages, market speculations, and cross-border market development, as well as counterfeiting, fraud and theft. Hence, the improvement of the modern market system and the effective functioning of the six aspects is still a long and arduous process.

(5) The six aspects of the vertical system of modern market are influencing or will soon influence all fields of the horizontal system of modern market. That is to say, the modern market system, which is gradually becoming complete over the course of history, will play a role not only in industrial economy, which is the economic foundation across the world, but also in urban economy and international economy (including deep-sea economy and space economy) gradually with the development and utilization of various generative resources. Different fields and different types of commodity economy, factor economy and project economy have produced different participants, which require the continuous improvement and perfection of the functions of the six aspects of the vertical system of modern market, which in turn requires the continuous improvement and perfection of contemporary economic theories, in particular, modern market theory.

3 Efficient Market Division

The concept of an efficient market was first proposed by Eugene Fama in 1970. Fama believed that when the prices of securities can fully reflect the information available to investors, the securities market is an efficient market, where investors can only expect the normal return rate corresponding to the investment risk no matter what securities are chosen randomly.

Fama then put forward the three-level theory of efficient market, that is, according to the types of information available to investors, efficient market can be divided into three levels: weak efficient market, semi-strong efficient market and strong efficient market. In the weak efficient market, all the information of past prices is already fully reflected in the current prices, so technical analysis analyzing the information of historical prices by means of moving average and candlestick charts is ineffective.

Besides information of previous prices in the securities market, the semi-strong efficient market also includes all the public information available in the news media, such as the annual and quarterly reports from the companies issuing securities; basic analysis relying on public information such as the financial statements of enterprises is also ineffective. The information in the strong efficient market includes not only all public information, but also all insider information, such as internal information held by senior managers in enterprises. If the strong efficient market holds water, all the above information would already be fully reflected in the current prices, then even investors holding insider information cannot continuously earn abnormal returns.

As a result, Fama put forward the premise for efficient market, that the Efficient Market Hypothesis presumes a perfect market. Firstly, there is no friction in the whole market, that is, there is no transaction costs and taxes; all assets can be completely separated and traded without restrictive provisions. Secondly, the whole market is fully competitive, and all market participants are price takers. Thirdly, there is no information cost. Finally, all market participants receive information at the same time, and all of them are rational and pursue maximum utility.

However, in reality, these assumptions are very difficult to hold. The presence of market frictions indicates that a completely efficient market is impossible. Investors must also consider transaction costs, opportunity costs, taxes and other costs. All these make the premise of an efficient market difficult to be achieved and the Efficient Market Hypothesis difficult to apply in practice.

Here I won't comment on whether it is reasonable of Fama to define the strength of an efficient market with the amount of transaction information carried by prices. What I do agree with is his methodology of dividing modern market into strong efficient market, semi-strong efficient market and weak efficient market. I think that this methodology of division can be further transplanted from the securities market to the whole modern market economy. Based on the differences in the growth and maturity levels of their market systems across the world, and the achievement of their functions of the six subsystems of the vertical system of modern market, efficient market can be divided into three levels: Markets in which only exist market factor system and market organization system belong to weak efficient markets. Such was the case in the market development of the United States from its founding in 1776–1890. On the basis of market factor system and market organization system, if a nation gradually establishes and improves the market legal system and market supervision system, it belongs to the semi-strong efficient market. The market development of the United States from 1890 to 1990 went with this type. On the basis of semi-strong efficient market, only when a nation establishes and improves the market environment system and market infrastructure can it belong to the strong efficient market. The market development and growth of the United States since the 1990s was in accordance with this trend.

The division into "strong", "semi-strong" and "weak" efficient markets based on the degree of maturity and completeness of the six subsystems of the vertical system of modern market is an extension of and reference to the methodology employed by Fama in dividing efficient markets. Not only can it reflect the original picture and genuine progress of the history of market economy across the world, it can also define clearly the different market types, guide the practice of market economy across the world, as well as evaluate its effectiveness scientifically. Constructing modern market systems and improving market functions play important roles in promoting economic development, urban construction and social livelihood, thus nations across the world are actively exploring and striving for breakthroughs in this field.

4 Re-understanding Market Failure

"Market failure" is a concept that originates from neoclassical economics, so current analysis of market failure mainly focuses on the field of industrial economy. Through the theoretical analysis of the functional structure of the six aspects of the vertical system of modern market in this chapter, and the case study analyzing the historical process of the growth and development of the modern market system in the United States, we can see that firstly, the improvement of market rules lags far behind the historical progress. During the early economic development after its founding in 1776, the mainstream United States concurred with the concept of laissez-faire. The United States at this stage was mainly establishing and improving the market factor system and market organization system. After 1890, the United States promulgated the first anti-monopoly law; particularly after the Great Depression and the world economic crisis in 1929–1933, the market legal system and market supervision system of the United States were gradually improved. Since the 1990s, faced with mixed operations and the explosive development of network technology, information and communication means, the market environment system and market infrastructure of the United States were gradually improved. As can be seen, the integrity and order of the functions of six aspects in the vertical system of modern market, as well as the formation of the complete market mechanism and market rules, have lagged far behind the actual historical progress of the market economy in the United States over the past two hundred years. The complete market function of the six aspects of the vertical system of modern market, both in theory and practice, has not yet been fully recognized and utilized till this day, which cannot but objectively lead to market failure. Among such lags in market rules, the lag in market legal and supervision systems is particularly prominent. It can be said that during the development of the United States from a fully competitive market to a monopolistic competitive market, to an oligopolistic market, and then to a fully monopolistic market, the legal and supervision systems of the United States have been taking a "crisis-oriented" "upgrading by patches" path of "patching and filling holes". Till this day, as the monopolistic competitive market in the United States develops towards the oligopolistic market, there still exist many disputes both in theory and practice on how to effectively regulate the oligopoly market by law. Being important parts of the vertical system of modern market, the legal and supervision systems are indispensable links in a complete market mechanism. Legal supervision measures like "patching and filling holes" of the United States are unable to create an open, fair and just market environment for various kinds of investors, which will also inevitably lead to market failure. Secondly, the realization of social public demand has always lagged behind the satisfaction of the interests of market subjects (that is, manufacturers or other investors). The market produces competition, and competition promotes equilibrium; but in reality, this equilibrium is mainly firm equilibrium, that is, the firm's short- or long-term equilibrium in product and price, cost and benefit, and supply and demand. The balance between social public demand and the interests of firms is basically non-existent. Social public interests are mainly guaranteed by the secondary distributions of governments across the world. The market subjects' protection of their interests may cause barriers, which will also lead to market failure. Due to the above reasons, it can be said that the fragility of the modern market economy system and market failure have become normal.

In reality, there always exist disputes on whether the industrial economy needs the government to formulate industrial policies to "plan, guide, support, coordinate, supervise and manage". The consensus is that in areas where the market fails to function, the government is required to play an active role. Such are areas of market failures. For example, Joseph Stiglitz, 2001 Nobel Prize winner in Economics, put forward "Creating a learning society" in 2014, focusing on the latest discoveries of market failure in economics. His views were that firstly, innovative activities (whether imitative or autonomous) have strong positive externalities, even become public goods of the whole industry in some cases, and result in limited incentives for enterprises. Secondly, information search and dissemination are also public goods in nature, so it is difficult to ensure their full provisions by relying solely on market mechanism. Finally, in the initial developmental stages of emerging industries, there exists a situation of insufficient market or even a total lack of market, which involves not only the market of their own products, but also the market of related inputs. Hence, in order to promote the development of emerging industries, non-market forces are required to play an active role to encourage innovation, provide information and foster markets; government intervention is the most important non-market force with significant effects. Therefore, professor Stiglitz suggested that government intervention may make up for market shortage and rectify market failure specifically in the following ways: (1) industrial and trade policies, which will help promote knowledge accumulation and dissemination within the industry; (2) fiscal and financial policies, which are the prerequisites for the implementation of industrial policies; (3) investment policies: Through subsidies, governments promote the production and proliferation of knowledge; (4) the construction of intellectual property rights system, which provides positive incentives to the individuals who discover, produce and proliferate knowledge. Thus, in order to promote the development of a "learning society", industrial policies are indispensable.[2] Relevant professors of Peking University have also acknowledged the necessities of industrial policies, and put forward five optimum conditions for the exploration and implementation of industrial policies: (1) Industrial policies must conform to the market and follow the trends. (2) Encourage competition. This is consistent with the Theory of Industrial Policy and Competition proposed by Philippe Aghion, master of the new endogenous economic growth theory. (3) Intervene cautiously. The government is not the pilot in developers' fantasy, but should be a down-to-earth servant, and the key to becoming a good servant is to accurately pinpoint the areas that need service. (4) There must be an exit mechanism, and there is a need for political economics to study the industrial policy exit mechanism. (5) Establish evaluation systems. The establishment of a reasonable policy evaluation system and accountability system is in itself a difficult problem and topic in political economics.[3] As seen, Stiglitz and other scholars still believe that the government and the market are isolated from each other, and that market failures and policy measures to remedy market failures still exist mainly in the area of industrial economy. It should be said that this view represents the mainstream opinion on market failure held by the world's economists today.

However, I hold the view that the various theoretical and practical problems in the economic development of the world today are not problems of the market or market economy, but due to a lack of modern market theory and the imperfection of the modern market economy. Developments in reality require a new economic system. As previously analyzed, the horizontal system of modern market includes the field of industrial resources, the field of urban resources which is being continuously developed, and the field of international resources (such as space resources and deep-sea resources, etc.), which is to be developed; the vertical system of modern market includes six major subsystems, namely, the market factor system, the market organization system, the market legal system, the market supervision system, the market environment system, and the market infrastructure. Horizontal and vertical systems integrate into a complete modern market system; the full realization of the functions of the six subsystems leads to the formation of a complete modern market mechanism. Henceforth, within this modern market system structure, there exist three types of market failures. The first is "defective market mechanism" failure. It is mainly embodied in the presently vigorously discussed industrial economy. As described previously, the effective attainment of the functions of the six aspects of the vertical system of modern market requires integrity and order. If defects and deficiencies exist in their functions, the fragility of the modern market system will manifest, and the biases of the development of the six subsystems will also lead to different fragilities. This type of market failure often manifests itself at various stages of economic development across the world. The second is "void in market mechanism" failure. This often occurs in the investment, development and construction of new generative resources. Traditional economic theory lacks the concepts of "resource generation" and "generative resources", and hence has difficulties dealing with the development and operation of urban economy with the investment and construction of infrastructure as the main content. Theories on industrial economy fall into contradictions here, blame the government instead for intervening in the market, and lead to a lack of guidance by economic theories on the investment, development and construction of new generative resources (including space economy, ocean economy and others, which will be developed vigorously in the future) across the world. The market operation mechanism is absent here. The third is "market mechanism barrier" failure. As is known from above, whether industrial economy or the investment and development economy of resource generation, they must adhere to the modern market mechanism, that is, the six subsystems of the vertical system of modern market should fully function. However, as the subjects in industrial economy or the subjects in the investment and development of resource generation are driven by interests, man-made barriers that violate market rules are easily caused, thereby hindering the openness, fairness and justice of the market.

Various fields in the horizontal system of modern market need to adhere to the rules of the six subsystems of the vertical system of modern market. Within the commodity, factor and project markets, the price, supply and demand, competition, and other mechanisms exert their influences, so that competitors obey market rules in the structure of the six major functions and principles of market allocation of resources, to fulfill market openness, fairness and justice. Henceforth, only by pinpointing the types of market failure can the right remedies be prescribed, effects of market allocation of resources fully exerted, and functions of governments better effected at the same time.

Notes

1. "It Is an Opportune Time Now to Conduct 'Aerospace' as a Big Business", *Nanfang Daily*, Oct. 31, 2016.
2. Gu Xin. "Rediscover Market Failure: Stiglitz, the Nobel Laureate, Talks About Industrial Policy", The Paper, Jan. 5, 2017, https://www.thepaper.cn/newsDetail_forward_1594001.
3. Ibid.

Chapter 7
Mature Effective Governments

1 The Types of Effective Governments

Through the analysis of the modern market economy in Chap. 6, we can figure out three levels of implications behind the "market". Firstly, the rational core of the market—market rules, in the field of industrial economy or resource generation, as "an invisible hand", widely play a role in the operating mechanism of commodities, factors, project prices, supply and demand, competition and others. Secondly, the market as a platform—The market in terms of circulation includes all kinds of tangible regional markets and intangible network markets, as well as all kinds of commodities, factors, projects, talents, technology and funds (including foreign exchange and others) that are circulated and traded in them, the production, circulation, transaction and consumption of which are constantly cycling under the guidance of the "invisible hand". Thirdly, the operation conditions of the market—The six subsystems of the vertical system of modern market are the basic conditions for the complete and orderly operation of the market, which guarantee the open, fair and just operation of market rules. Of course, if the functions and structures of these six subsystems are not complete in a certain field or at a certain stage, the market can still work, and market rules can still function; but the deficiencies of a certain subsystem will bring about fragility in the market, and lead to economic crisis and even worldwide economic depression caused by market failure, and eventually the market will be destroyed or even rebuilt.

Based on the degree of maturity and completeness of the six subsystems of the vertical modern market system, the market economy that consists only of the market factor system and market organization system is called "weak efficient market"; based on this, the market economy that gradually improves its market legal system and market supervision system is called "semi-strong efficient market"; the market economy that further establishes and improves its market environment system and market infrastructure is called "strong efficient market". What needs to be clarified in this chapter is the theory of the three types of effective governments that corre-

Y. Chen, *New Economic Engine: Effective Government and Efficient Market*, China Academic Library, https://doi.org/10.1007/978-981-15-2922-1_7

sponds to the theory of the three types of efficient markets. There also exist three types of effective governments: "weak effective government", "semi-strong effective government" and "strong effective government".

In Chap. 3, we talk about the three kinds of resources that exist in the real economic operation across the world—operational resources, non-operational resources and quasi-operational resources. As discussed in Chap. 4, for operational resources corresponding to the industrial economy in reality, governments should follow the principles of "planning and guidance; support and coordination; supervision and management" to make policies; for non-operational resources corresponding to the livelihood economy in reality, governments should follow the principles of "general underpinning, fairness and justice, and effective promotion" to make policies; for quasi-operational resources corresponding to urban economy (in its narrow sense) in reality, governments should follow the principles of "participating in market competition, maintaining market order, and following market rules" to make policies. In Chap. 5, we talk about government's competition in broad and narrow senses. In a broad sense, governments promote the competitions of operational resources through supporting policies, which can invigorate the industrial economy and make it develop coordinately, thereby elevating the level of the industrial economy of the region. By promoting the competitions of non-operational resources through supporting policies, governments can promote the growth of livelihood economy, maintain social stability, and optimize the investment and development environment of the region. By promoting the competitions of quasi-operational resources through supporting policies, governments can push the investment, development and construction of urban economy, and promote the comprehensive and sustainable development of the social economy of the region.

Corresponding to the above analysis, we can divide effective governments into three categories. The first category is governments that are only concerned with the allocation of non-operational resources (that is, social public welfare resources related to the livelihood) and the related policies, which could be called weak effective government. This category of governments confine their functions to the basic social public welfare guarantee, and have neither a clear understanding of nor actions on the allocation of operational resources and related policies, and have neither a clear definition of nor measures on the participation in the competition of quasi-operational resources and related policies. The second category is governments that are only concerned with the allocation of non-operational resources and operational resources and the related policies, which could be called semi-strong effective governments. In addition to performing basic public functions such as social security, this category of governments also look at the state of market operation. When the operation of the market is failing, this category of governments can use policy measures to mobilize effective demand or effective supply, implement macro-control and intervention to prevent the economy from falling into excessive depression and causing heavy losses and damage. At the same time, such governments can formulate economic strategies, plan and guide the industrial layout, support and adjust production and operation, and supervise market competition under the principles of openness, fairness and justice, regulate and control prices, control the unemployment rate, so as to promote the dynamic equilibrium between aggregate supply and aggregate demand. However, their understanding of quasi-operational resources is vague, leading to unclear definitions and policies, inadequate measures and poor results. The third category is governments that not only pay attention to the allocations of non-operational resources and operational resources and related policies, but also participate in and promote the allocations of quasi-operational resources and related policies, which could be called strong effective governments. This category of governments exert guidance, regulation, forewarning and other functions during economic development, and by relying on market mechanism and using measures on planning, investment, consumption, price, taxation, interest rate, exchange rate, law, and others, bring about value, institutional, organizational and technological innovations. Through the effective allocation of operational resources, such governments improve the economic development environment; through the effective allocation of non-operational resources, they enhance the vitality and coordination of economic development; through the effective allocation of quasi-operational resources, they form the leading edge to promote the comprehensive, scientific and sustainable development of the social economy. The strong effective government mode is the route to success for nations in their competition in the global market system.

2 Government Foresighted Leading (GFL)

In my opinion, the strong effective government should lead with foresight. Enterprises do the things they should do, whilst governments do the things enterprises cannot do or cannot do well. Neither of them can be absent nor vacant. Government foresighted leading (GFL) is to adhere to market rules and rely on market forces, to guide, regulate and forewarn the industrial economy, to allocate, participate in and maintain the order of the urban economy, and to guarantee, underpin and elevate the livelihood economy. This requires the government to utilize measures of planning, investment, consumption, price, taxation, interest rate, exchange rate, law and others to bring about policy, value, institutional, organizational and technological innovations, to effectively promote supply-side or demand-side structural reform, form the leading edge in economic growth, and promote scientific and sustainable development.

As can be seen, the prerequisite for government foresighted leading is to rely on market mechanism, that is, the market decides the allocation of resources. The principle behind government foresighted leading is that the governments guide, regulate and forewarn the industrial economy; allocate, participate in and maintain order of the urban economy; and guarantee, underpin and promote the livelihood economy. The means of government foresighted leading include planning, investment, consumption, price, taxation, interest rate, exchange rate, law and others, and bringing about value, institutional, organizational and technological innovations herewith. The purpose of government foresighted leading is to promote structural reform on the supply-side or the demand-side, to form the leading edge for economic growth, and to attain scientific and sustainable development.

In theory, the essential differences between government foresighted leading and Keynesian government intervention are: Firstly, the behavior occasions are different. Government foresighted leading is mainly manifested in top-level designing, planning and layout setting in advance, as opposed to Keynesian mid- and post-intervention, and the policy effects are also different. Secondly, the regulation emphasis and policy measures are different. The emphasis of Keynesianism is on the demand-side, whereas the emphasis of government foresighted leading is on the guidance, adjustment and supervision of industrial resources, urban resources and livelihood resources; Keynesianism mainly uses fiscal policies to intervene in the economy, whereas the policy measures of government foresighted leading are all-rounded and applied throughout the whole process, and constantly innovating and developing. Thirdly, and more importantly, the government's functions are different. The theory on government foresighted leading suggests that governments are one of the subjects in market competition, the mature market economy is "strong effective government plus strong efficient market", and the governments' competition in the market economy cannot be neglected; whereas Keynesianism endeavors to exert the effects of government intervention in practice, and yet in theory, excludes the government from the market. This incomplete market theory and government economic behavior rendered Keynesian theory and its practice limited. Fourthly, the operation modes are different. The main characteristics of classical economics and neoclassical economics are the market (the invisible hand) and a focus on supply (commodity, price, supply regulation). The main characteristics of Keynesian economics are government intervention and a focus on demand (driven by a troika of investment, consumption, and exports). Whereas the theory on government foresighted leading is related to classical and neoclassical economics and Keynesian economics, there are also differences. Its mode of operation is that governments' lead (intervention) integrates with emphasis on supply, which not only ensures the economic principle that the market decides the allocation of resources, but also requires governments to exert their effects of guidance, adjustment and supervision during the process.

On the practical level, most nations in the world are at the critical period of economic transition, social transformation or exploring and overcoming the "Middle Income Trap"; promoting industrial transformation and urban upgrading through government foresighted leading has become one of the development routes explored by nations across the world. With my experience of serving as secretary of the CPC Municipal Committee and mayor in Foshan City of Guangdong Province around 2010 as an example, the following discussions attempt to explore the specific measures taken by the government leading with foresight.

In 2009, Foshan City, with an area of 3,797.72 km^2, a resident population of 6.8747 million and a regional GDP of RMB 485.288 billion yuan, ranked 11th amongst large and medium-sized cities in China, with a per capita GDP of RMB 72,167 yuan (about USD 11,000 in that year). Its industrial development entered the late stage of industrialization and the early stage of post-industrialization. Under the new situation of industrial transformation, accelerated urbanization and enhanced internationalization, a very urgent problem for Foshan was how to accelerate industrial transformation and urban upgrading. Keeping in mind the realities, the Foshan Municipal Government conducted in-depth investigation, piloted and experimented five ways to promote industrial transformation and urban upgrading with various policies.

(1) "Double transfer" and "vacating cage to change birds": The Foshan Municipal Government actively implemented the "double transfer" (that is, industry transfer and labor force transfer) strategy, using bank loans, government discounts and financial guarantees to promote the "three batches" policy, realizing the "vacating cage to change birds" policy, and leading industries to accelerate their transformation. The specific measures of the so-called "three batches" are as follows:

Firstly, to close or transfer a batch of industries: The government accelerated the elimination of outdated production capacities, shut down or renovated more than 1,200 high-pollution and high-energy-consumption enterprises in ceramics, cement, bleaching and dyeing, aluminum profile casting, glass and other industries, among whom 649 enterprises with high energy consumption and pollution were directly closed down. At the same time, the government guided the transfer of labor-intensive enterprises to less developed areas. In recent years, around 460 projects of Foshan City were transferred to industrial parks in some mountainous cities of Guangdong Province, which not only made room for the industrial transformation and upgrading of Foshan, but also provided the impetus for the economic development of the areas accepting these projects.

Secondly, to upgrade a batch of industries: The government promoted the integration of informatization and industrialization, and the match between service industries and manufacturing industries, and promoted the transformation of traditional industries into heavy, innovative and high-end industries. Take the ceramic industry as an example. In 2007, there were more than 400 manufacturing enterprises in Foshan; after three years of transformation and upgrading, all of the 50 enterprises retained achieved clean production and reengineering of their production process, thereby developing from production bases to multi-functional bases that entail headquarters and exhibition, R&D, logistics and information centers, etc. During these three years, ceramic output in Foshan City decreased by 40%, but output value and tax revenue increased by 33%, energy consumption decreased by 25%, and sulphur dioxide emissions decreased by 20%.

Thirdly, to cultivate a batch of industries: Through inviting and selecting investment, the government focused on optoelectronics, new materials, and modern service industries, cultivated new medicine, environmental protection and electric vehicle industries, and fostered the rapid formation of new energy (solar photovoltaic), new light source (liquid crystal displays) and other emerging industries. These measures have effectively reduced the proportion of traditional industries, and Foshan has become a national demonstration area for new industrialization industries and electronic information (photoelectric display) industries. At the same time, through the "Three-Outmoded Transformation" (outmoded towns, outmoded factories, outmoded villages), Foshan developed new cities, new industries and new communities, which not only improved the efficiency of land use, but also promoted industrial transformation, urban transformation and environmental reconstruction.

(2) Introducing large projects and promoting industrial upgrading: During the promotion of industrial transformation and urban upgrading, the Foshan Municipal Government paid attention to attracting investment, adopted policy measures to promote financial investment (such as private equity investment, venture investment and others), focused on leading projects in strategic emerging industries, advanced manufacturing industries and modern service industries, and through investing in and introducing large projects of international standards, quickly cultivated new industrial clusters and seized the strategic commanding heights in industrial development. Examples are as follows. Through the introduction of the Qimei electronic flat panel display module project, manufacturers of upstream parts such as chips, panels, molds, and plastics, and downstream TV manufacturers will be attracted to invest, forming a complete industrial chain of LCD flat panel displays, and inspiring the upgrading of household appliances industry in Foshan. The introduction of the IRICO OLCD project inspired the development of the third generation of display industry. The introduction of FAW-Volkswagen project inspired the whole auto parts manufacturing industry to develop into industrial clusters and complete industrial chains.

During this period, Foshan ushered in 87 investment projects from 47 of the Fortune Global 500 enterprises, and 167 investment projects from 99 of the top 500 enterprises in China, formed a batch of key enterprises with leading status in their respective industries in China, which played a leading role in technology, standards and brands, and effectively elevated the industrial structure and urban development standards of Foshan City.

(3) Promoting scientific and technological progress and independent innovation: During this period, there were more than 347,000 enterprises registered in the industrial and commercial administrative bureau of Foshan, of which more than 100,000 were industrial enterprises, but only more than 2,200 enterprises had an output value of more than RMB 100 million yuan, while more than 99% were small and medium-sized enterprises with an output value of less than RMB 100 million yuan. In view of the industrial structure, the Foshan Municipal Government promoted the integrated development of finance, science and technology, and industry, constantly innovated and formulated guidance and incentive policies of foundation consolidation, brand creation, patent registration, standard formulation, and brand exports, encouraged and supported enterprises to independently establish industry standards, national standards, and even international standards, form their own core technologies, and based on their own brands, patents and standards, entrust other enterprises to make OEM products for Foshan enterprises.

During this period, the Foshan Municipal Government spent RMB 1 billion yuan annually as direct incentives in guiding enterprises to strengthen scientific and technological investment and independent innovation. In 2008, this measure led enterprises to invest more than RMB 22 billion yuan, achieved an increase of 47%; in 2009, in spite of the influence of the international financial crisis, this measure still led enterprises to invest more than RMB 30.8 billion yuan, achieving an increase of 39%. Through such policy measures, the Foshan Municipal Government promoted scientific and technological progress and independent innovation, and took the lead in industrial transformation and urban upgrading. Foshan was awarded one of the "Top 10 Cities to Build Innovation-oriented Country", "Chinese Brand Economic City" and "Capital of Chinese Brands", and the only model city of national famous trademark and famous brand amongst prefecture-level cities in Guangdong Province. In around 2012, Foshan accumulated 130,000 patent applications and 86,000 patent authorizations, both ranking first amongst China's prefecture-level cities; and 42 Famous Trademarks of China and 65 China Top Brand products, ranking fourth amongst China's large and medium-sized cities.

(4) Using financial policies and constructing industrial leading positions: By the strength of capital and financial policy measures, the Foshan Municipal Government promoted the effective integration of enterprises and capital markets to get bigger and stronger. Internally, Foshan implemented three financial development plans: Firstly, through the "463" Plan[1] to promote the public listing of enterprises, the number of listed enterprises in Foshan increased from 13 in 2007 to 26 in 2010, and a listing echelon comprising 102 enterprises was formed. At the same time, governmental support for mergers and acquisitions also promoted the industrial transformation and upgrading. Secondly, through cultivating equity investment funds, small and medium-sized enterprise guarantee funds, funds for talents, etc., the effective match between industry and finance was promoted. During this period, Foshan had 15 funds, and equity investment funds amounted to about RMB 1.2 billion yuan, amongst which the guiding funds by local governments amounted to RMB 126 million yuan and drove about RMB 1.1 billion yuan of private capital. Enterprises' listing on SME and GEM boards were accelerated, with 45 enterprises ready to file applications and more than 30 getting pre-listing tutoring or ready to reorganize. Thirdly, through financial innovation, such as the development of rural banks, micro-loan companies, and others, financial support was provided for industrial transformation and upgrading.

Externally, capitalizing on the opportunity of establishing Foshan as the only model city of industrial cluster and effective capital market operation in China by the United Nations Industrial Development Organization, Foshan actively attracted foreign banks into the Guangdong Hi-tech Service Zone for Financial Institutions located in Foshan. During this period, 28 projects signed contract of entry, and total investment amounted to RMB 6,579 million yuan. Since the "Supplement VI to the Mainland and Hong Kong Closer Economic Partnership Arrangement (CEPA)"[2] took effect in October 2009, four Hong Kong-funded banks have been stationed in Foshan. These measures guaranteed strong support from the capital market for the transformation and upgrading of enterprises, assisted enterprises to establish a management mechanism in line with international standards, and in particular, enabled private enterprises to establish a modern enterprise system, achieve transformation, and become more vigorous, with private enterprises contributing 61.8% to the economic growth of the entire city.

(5) Promoting the integration of informatization, industrialization, urbanization and internationalization as well as the construction of intelligent Foshan: Following closely the global wave of the information technology revolution and construction of intelligent cities, the Foshan Municipal Government promoted the integration of informatization, industrialization, urbanization and internationalization and the construction of intelligent Foshan through financial policy means, and led the future development of the city. This became a strategic breakthrough in the industrial transformation and upgrading throughout the "12th Five-Year Plan" period of Foshan City. The specific measures are as follows:

Firstly, integrate informatization with industrialization, to vigorously cultivate technology associated with informatization such as photoelectric display and radio frequency identification, as well as emerging industries such as the Internet of Things, industrial design and service outsourcing, and to transform and upgrade traditional industries. For example, there were more than 1,700 furniture enterprises in Longjiang Town, Shunde District, but only a few of these had an output value exceeding RMB 100 million yuan. The Wision Group adopted three-dimensional visual effect technology, provided personalized customization, changed the sales mode of "stocks awaiting purchase" of traditional furniture enterprises, and changed the buyers' market into the sellers' market. Within a mere two or three years, the scale of sales exceeded RMB 300 million yuan. For another example, the Midea Group used the Internet of Things technology to transform and upgrade household appliances to intelligent appliances, replaced traditional appliances and brought about a new revolution in the household appliance industry.

Secondly, integrate informatization with urbanization, to actively explore and promote the integration of telecommunication network, television network and the Internet, and develop intelligent services and management systems such as intelligent transportation, intelligent public order, intelligent urban management, intelligent education, intelligent medical treatment, intelligent culture, intelligent commerce, intelligent government affairs, and others, so as to form the ubiquitous "U Foshan" to attain the three major leaps from management to service, from governance to operation, from partial application to integrated service, turning Foshan into an intelligent city conducive to living, commerce and development.

Thirdly, integrate informatization with internationalization. On the micro level, the government guides enterprises to build internationalized R&D, production, sales and service systems based on information technology such as the Internet of Things, the Internet, radio frequency identification and others, and to improve their capability to exploit the international market, e.g., to turn Foshan into an international purchasing center for ceramics and household appliances based on the Internet of Things. On the macro level, through the construction of cross-departmental, cross-sectoral, and cross-regional "electronic ports", that is, customs clearance information platform, the government provided enterprises with "one-stop" customs clearance services such as electronic payment, logistics distribution, electronic customs declaration, electronic inspection, and others, paving the "highway" for enterprises to enter the international market.

During the first half of 2010, Foshan's regional GDP amounted to RMB 265.1 billion yuan, with an increase of 13.8%. The proportion of advanced manufacturing industries, high-tech industries and modern service industries was increasing continuously, gradually possessing the excellent structure of a modern industrial system and forming the development trend of advanced cities. The practice of Foshan City has proven that government foresighted leading by effectively using policy measures is a victorious route to promote the transformation of local industries and urban upgrading, and can strongly promote the scientific and sustainable development of regional economy.[3]

3 Innovation is Competitiveness

For social and economic development, strong effective government should lead with foresight; government foresighted leading is the key to regional competition and development. Competition needs innovation; innovation is competitiveness, and sustainable innovation is sustainable competitiveness. Government innovation is the core of regional government competition across the world. As observed from the innovation level, government needs value innovation, organizational innovation, institutional innovation, and technological innovation.

First of all, "value foresighted leading" is an important competitiveness when regional economic development is at the factor-driven stage. At this stage, economic growth across the world depends mainly on the input of production factors such as labor force, land and other natural resources. This is a simple expansion in quantity and competition for resources and prices, and is prone to excessive plundering of production factors, low productivity, lagging technology, resource exhaustion, brain drain, intensification of social contradictions and other problems. Hence, at this stage, the thoughts, directions and modes of development are decisive. Advanced values determine the future setups and trends of the region. The value innovation of the regional government becomes the focus of regional competition, and this includes the overall grasp and control of the three types of regional resources, the positioning of future development strategies for the region, the overall planning of the future development mode of the region, and solutions to the development mode and development motive at the level of top-level design. Hence, when regional economic development is at the factor-driven stage, sound value foresighted leading, and the coordinated, green and open development of the three types of resources will promote the stable and coordinated growth of the regional economy.

Secondly, "organizational foresighted leading" is the key to competition when regional economic development is at the investment-driven stage. When regional development is at the investment-driven stage, the main means of regional competition across the world are to expand the scale of investment to stimulate economic growth. On one hand, due to the existence of the investment multiplier effect, investment can promote economic expansion by multiple times, which is also proven by Keynes' effective demand theory. Hence, investment is an important means to increase effective demand and GDP. During periods of regional economic downturn, in particular, governments can reverse the trend of economic decline by increasing investment to help turn the economy around. However, on the other hand, simple pursuit of the short-term effects of stimulation through investment is prone to "investment hunger" and "investment dependence", and will cause a series of symptoms such as economic ups and downs, backward technological innovation abilities, and others. Hence, at the investment-driven stage of regional economic development, innovation in organizational management becomes the key, that is, the government needs to regulate the investment and management of the three types of regional resources, strengthen rapid response capabilities of the organization, get closer to the market, serve the enterprises, develop network structure and matrix structure, reduce management levels, so as to effectively enhance the effects of investment with greater efficiency and flexibility. Hence, when regional economic development is at the investment-driven stage, sound organizational foresighted leading is the key to the stable and orderly development of the regional economy, and to winning in regional competition.

Thirdly, "institutional and technological foresighted leading" are the winning points in competition when regional economic development is at the innovation-driven stage. The innovation-driven stage is the most explosive stage of economic development, when both the allocation of the three types of resources and social economic development have started the leap from quantitative change to qualitative change and the growth in social economy has achieved a breakthrough in the entire process and in all the factors. At this stage, technological innovation is the core driving force, whilst institutional innovation is the fundamental guarantee of technological innovation. Technological innovation expedites new formats, new products, new industries and new models; institutional innovation guarantees and promotes the integration and innovation of science and technology, finance and industries; together, they make possible the sustainability of innovation-driven models. Henceforth at this stage, sound technological and institutional foresighted leading becomes important means of regional competition.

Finally, "comprehensive foresighted leading" is the inevitable choice in competition when regional economic development is at the wealth-driven stage. If regional economy development across the world truly follows the tracks of factor-driven, investment-driven, innovation-driven and wealth-driven, then at the wealth-driven stage, individual creativity will be brought into full play, people's work and life will be fully balanced, the three major industries will change rapidly with each passing day, the entire society's consciousness of resources and environment will become stronger and stronger, and new economic development models and personal growth models will be constantly brought forth, and these require governments not only to carry out value innovation, technological innovation, organizational innovation, and institutional innovation, but also to realize comprehensive foresighted leading, scientific and orderly allocation of the three types of regional resources, so as to ensure the long-term advantages in regional competition. As economic development at this stage is flexible, rapid and diverse, it requires governmental systems, policies and measures to coordinate with it. Only in this way, can regional governments grasp the pulse of the wealth-driven era, take leads in the value orientation, and maintain the economic vitality. Hence, at this stage, sustained innovation and foresighted leading in all aspects, in the entire process, and in all factors will be an inevitable choice for regional competition.

4 Government Failure Revisited

As mentioned earlier, in *The Wealth of Nations*, Adam Smith proposed the theories of "the invisible hand" and "the government as night watchman", which were carried forward by classical economics and neoclassical economics. Faced with the British economic depression, unemployment of workers and the great economic crisis of 1929–1933 in the United States and even the world, Keynes put forward a series of propositions and specific measures on state intervention in the economy. Since then, government's intervention in and regulation of the economy has become an important policy of Western nations, and has been further expanded by post-Keynesianism. At the end of the 1970s, the economy of Western nations fell into stagflation; the Phillips curve could not explain the stagflation phenomenon of increased unemployment, economic stagnation and high inflation rates existing simultaneously. The concept of "government failure" spontaneously emerged and became the focus of mainstream economic research.

According to traditional economics, government failure, also known as government defeat or government defect, refers to the situation that individual demand for public goods is not well satisfied, while the public sector tends to waste and abuse resources when providing public goods, resulting in excessive or inefficient public expenditure, and lack of efficiency in governmental activities or intervention measures. Or in other words, the government makes decisions that reduce or fail to improve economic efficiency. Its main manifestations include: Firstly, due to the constraints of competency and other objective factors, government's intervention in economic activities cannot meet expectations. Secondly, government's intervention in economic activities meets expectations, but its inefficiency or high costs rendered resources inadequately or ineffectively utilized. Thirdly, government's intervention in economic activities meets expectations with a rather high efficiency, but it brings about unexpected adverse side effects. Fourthly, some externalities or international economic and trade problems cannot be solved by a single government, such as pollution from nuclear use, international trade disputes, and others. The main reasons for government failure include: firstly, the deficiencies in public decision-making lead to the inefficiency of public policies or even deviation from public objectives; secondly, the inefficient public policy implementation results in policy failure; thirdly, the uncertainty of public policies themselves results in intervention failure; fourthly, government failure caused by rent-seeking; and lastly, government failure is caused by defects inherent in the process of governmental regulation of the economy.

I will not comment here on the accuracies of the above views, or whether they are complete; instead, based on the practice of effective allocation of the three types of resources across the world, I shall attempt to analyze and evaluate the roles of regional governments in resource allocation and economic development.

The three types of resources exist in each nation or region, and how these resources are allocated defines the type of effective government. As mentioned above, for non-operational resources (livelihood economy), government's policies should follow the principles of "fairness and justice, general underpinning and effective promotion"; for operational resources (industrial economy), government's policies should embody the principles of "planning and guidance; support and coordination; supervision and management"; for quasi-operational resources (urban economy, and even space economy, marine economy, and others), government's policies should follow the principles of "acting as not only competitors, but also allocators and supervisors". In the process of allocating the three types of resources, national or regional governments should make policies according to the different characteristics of the various resources in order to promote the balanced and rapid development of social economy. Such policies or government actions, are what is expected of effective governments. On this basis, according to the degree of perfection of the above-mentioned supporting policies, effective governments can be further categorized into weak effective government, semi-strong effective government and strong effective government.

Governments should be effective in the market economy, nevertheless, there exist in reality, three types of government failures: (1) The type of "inadequate livelihood economy": Such governments regard livelihood economy as a burden, without any general underpinning or effective promotion, nor consideration of the important effects that a fair and just foundation of livelihood has on building an investment environment that is stable, harmonious, and conducive to commerce, living, business and tourism. This type of government failure arises from governmental "lack of knowledge". (2) The type of "lack of industrial polices": This includes not only the lack of "planning, guidance and support" policies on the industrial economy, but also the lack of "coordination, supervision and management" policies on it. If regional governments are deficient in policies in both aspects as mentioned above, or only emphasize on one of the aspects, circumstances will arise where discipline is lacking or intervention is inappropriate. This type of government failure arises from governmental "misunderstanding". (3) The type of "void urban construction": For example, there are very few or even no policies and measures to promote regional economic growth through urban construction (investment in and construction of software and hardware infrastructure, and even the development and operation of intelligent cities).

Or some infrastructure investment and development does exist, but the scale is small and the layout is scattered; the government neither participates as one of the competitors nor acts as the main regulator to fully exert its regulatory effects. Or the government does participate in the competition, but does not adhere to the market rules. Instead it aims only for administrative performances, invests without regard to returns, focuses only on construction and neglects management, and considers only public welfare and neglects benefits. This will result in massive wastage of urban infrastructure, low-quality operation of urban construction, disorderly operation of urban management, etc. This type of government failure arises from governmental "ignorance".

Regional governments across the world have dual quasi-macro and quasi-micro attributes, so do governments in the integration of the global economy. Together with enterprises, they become the dual competitors in the market economic system. Governments need to face the problem of how to lead with foresight through value, technological, organizational and institutional innovations, avoid or reduce market failures, thereby accomplishing the best mode of "effective government plus efficient market" in the modern market economy. We should foster the organic combination of effective government and efficient market, and boost the overall, scientific and sustainable development of the global economy.

Notes

1. The "463" Plan: from 2008 on, to promote the shareholding system transformation or launch of public listing of at least 100 enterprises within four years, and the successful listing of 60 home or abroad, and to reach a gross financing of RMB 30 billion yuan.
2. The Supplement VI to CEPA, signed on May 9, 2009 and effective on Oct. 1 of the same year, aims to further enhance the level of economic and trade exchanges and cooperation between the mainland and the Hong Kong SAR. According to the supplement, the mainland shall further relax the market access conditions in 20 areas, namely, legal, construction, medical, research and development services, real estate, placement and supply services of personnel, printing, convention and exhibition, public utility, telecommunications, audiovisual, distribution, banking, securities, tourism, cultural, maritime transport, air transport, rail transport and individually owned stores. Many of the specific polices were piloted in Guangdong Province.
3. Song Jing. "Intelligent Foshan: Path of Transformation Under the Logic of Power Division", *China Nongovernmental Science Technology and Economy*, Vol. 7 (2011): 50–55.

Chapter 8
The Choices of Effective Government and Efficient Market Modes

1 Potential Economic Growth Rate and Real Economic Growth Rate

The vertical modern market system includes six aspects: market factor system, market organization system, market legal system, market supervision system, market environment system and market infrastructure. Economic resources across the world can be divided into three categories: operational resources, non-operational resources and quasi-operational resources. The different ways of matching the two result in different combination modes for effective government and efficient market in the market economy.

In order to clarify these different combination modes, the two indicators of potential economic growth rate and real economic growth rate ought to be analyzed first.

Potential economic growth rate refers to the highest growth rate of aggregate goods and services produced by a nation in the modern market system, or in other words, the highest economic growth rate that a nation can attain under the condition that various resources are allocated optimally. This includes two connotations. Firstly, the market is efficient, that is, the basic market functions (including market factor system and market organization system), the basic market order (including market legal system and market supervision system), and the foundation of the market environment (including market environment system and market infrastructure) in the modern market system are sound. Secondly, the government is effective, that is, operational resources, non-operational resources and quasi-operational resources can be effectively allocated, and matched with policies and systems by the government. As can be seen, potential economic growth rate is the growth rate that the government of a nation can achieve when it makes the best use of the three types of resources under a sound modern market system, and is the growth rate realized under the mode of "strong effective government plus strong efficient market".

Y. Chen, *New Economic Engine: Effective Government and Efficient Market*, China Academic Library, https://doi.org/10.1007/978-981-15-2922-1_8

The real economic growth rate is the percentage change in the value of a nation's Gross National Product (GNP) during a specific period of time, as compared to an earlier period. The GNP measured at current market prices of the end-period is the nominal economic growth rate, whereas the GNP measured at constant market prices of the base-period is the real economic growth rate. The real economic growth rate reflects the rate of real economic growth; it is a dynamic indicator of changes in the level of economic development in a nation within a certain period of time.

Due to differences in the degree of market development and government capabilities across the world, there exists the mode of "weak effective government plus weak efficient market", such as in most middle- or low-income nations, and the mode of "semi-strong effective government plus strong efficient market", such as in the United States today, and also the mode of "strong effective government plus semi-strong efficient market", such as in China at present, which still needs to further improve its market competition order, market credit system and market infrastructure. There exists a certain gap between the real economic growth rate in all these nations and the potential economic growth rate under the mode of "strong effective government and strong efficient market".

This gap is where the potential of economic growth across the world lies. The series of economic measures taken to bridge this gap are where the vitality of economic development across the world lies, and the series of policies or systems made to bridge this gap are where innovation for economic development across the world lies. A mature market economy equates strong effective government plus strong efficient market, which is the highest form of combination of governments and market, the best mode concluded from economic practice through constant exploration, and also the only route to the realization of the potential economic growth rate across the world.

In the real economy, situations often arise where aggregate social demand is less than aggregate social supply, or aggregate social demand is greater than aggregate social supply. We can start from the modes of effective government and efficient market, the six subsystems of the vertical market system, and the government's allocation of the three types of resources, to find the root causes of problems, and put forward the direction and basic route to their solution.

2 Washington Consensus and the Middle Income Trap

At the end of the 1980s, the world economy slipped into recession and economic growth rates across the world shrank, with inadequate impetus for economic growth, weak demand, and decreasing population growth rate. The economic globalization encountered twists and turns, the financial market was turbulent, and international trade and investment remained in a slump… Faced with such situations, in 1989, the American Institute for International Economics invited the International Monetary Fund, the World Bank, the Inter-American Development Bank, and others, to seminars in Washington D.C., and formed the so-called "Washington Consensus". The

Consensus is a set of ten policy measures: (1) fiscal policy discipline, with avoidance of large fiscal deficits and inflation rates, to stabilize macro economy; (2) redirection of public spending toward broad-based provision of key pro-growth, pro-poor services like primary education, primary health care and infrastructure investment; (3) tax reform, broadening the tax base and adopting moderate marginal tax rates; (4) interest rates that are market determined; (5) competitive exchange rates; (6) trade liberalization and opening up markets; (7) liberalization of inward foreign direct investment; (8) privatization of state enterprises; (9) deregulation; (10) legal security for property rights.

The core of the Washington Consensus is "minimal state and expedited privatization and liberalization". In theory, it advocates the implementation of a perfectly free market economy model to minimize the roles played by governments, and believes that as long as the market can allocate resources freely, economic growth can be attained. In terms of policies, its measures mainly include expediting the liberalization of the market, and domestic and foreign trade, expediting the privatization of state-owned enterprises, as well as reducing fiscal deficits, strictly restricting loans and issuance of currencies in order to achieve macroeconomic stability.

The original purpose of the Washington Consensus was to provide economic reform measures and countermeasures for Latin American countries that were mired in debt crisis, and to provide political and economic theoretical basis for Eastern European countries in transition. It should be said that during specific stages, the ten policy measures of the Washington Consensus did have certain effectiveness on stimulating the economic development of various nations. Nevertheless, these not only neglected the importance of improving the six subsystems of the market system, but also neglected the importance of governments across the world allocating the three types of economic resources, hence, falling into the "weak effective government plus weak efficient market" mode. In this mode, the government has basically no regulatory effects on the economy, the market development is not complete, the legal system is lacking, disorder prevails, and the market competition mechanism is often impeded. Such theoretical propositions, policy measures and modes will certainly not endure and fall into dilemma.

In 2006, the World Bank put forward the concept of "middle-income trap": Those middle-income economies, that is, the emerging markets, during the process of reaching high-income levels, after breaking through the "poverty trap" of per capita GDP of USD 1,000, would rapidly move to the "take-off stage" of USD 1,000 to USD 3,000 (per capita GDP). However, when the per capita GDP reaches about USD 3,000, the contradictions that have been accumulating during the rapid development will erupt all at once, and the renewal of mechanism and systems of these economies will reach a bottleneck. Contradictions are difficult to overcome, and the economic growth slows down or falls into stagnation, that is, the stage of middle-income trap.

At this stage, these countries are facing two dilemmas: On the one hand, the costs of resources, raw materials, labor force, capital, and management remain high. On the other hand, they have difficulties innovating due to lack of core cutting-edge technologies, and are stuck in the middle and low ends of the industrial chain without competitiveness. The decline or stagnation of economic growth leads to further employment difficulties, shortage of social public services, fragile financial system, polarization between the rich and poor, rampant corruption, lack of faith, social unrest and other issues. Consequently, these countries hover in the middle-income stage for long periods, unable to become high-income economies.

Latin American countries that adhered to the Washington Consensus to promote economic reform have also become typical examples of countries caught in the middle-income trap. Argentina's per capita GDP already exceeded USD 1,000 in 1964, and rose to over USD 8,000 by the late 1990s; however, it fell to over USD 2,000 in 2002, and then rose again to over USD 12,000 in 2014. Mexico's per capita GDP already reached USD 1,000 in 1973, but in 2016 was just over USD 8,000. After forty years it was still classified as an upper middle class country. Many countries in Latin America are similar, failing to cross the USD 15,000 (per capita GDP) threshold for developed countries despite their repeated efforts over the past twenty or thirty years and a lot of ups and downs.

We can use Argentina as a typical case to analyze the "nidus" of stagnation in Latin American countries. Firstly, there were huge fluctuations in the real economic growth rate. During the 45 years from 1963 to 2008, Argentina's per capita GDP grew at an average annual rate of only 1.4% and saw negative growth for 16 years. In 1963, Argentina's per capita GDP was USD 842, which already reached the level of middle-and high-income countries at that time, but after 45 years, it only grew to USD 8,236, still at the same level. Secondly, the technology engine was weak. In terms of the proportion of R&D expenditure in GDP, Argentina's was 0.41% in 2003, ranked beyond top 40 in the world. In terms of R&D personnel, in 2006, there were only 1.1 R&D personnel in every 1,000 people in Argentina. In terms of labor quality, in 2007, the proportion of labor force with college education and above in Argentina was 29.5%, with no obvious advantage. Thirdly, it suffered severe polarization between the rich and the poor, and prominent social conflicts. In terms of Gini Coefficient, Argentina was around 0.45 in the mid-1980s, close to 0.5 in the late 1990s and 0.51 in 2007. Problems of inequitable distribution are reflected not only in property income, but also in wage grade. Coupled with underdeveloped urban infrastructure and public services, Argentina's public security worsened continuously, and social conflicts were prominent. Finally, government management was ineffective. There was long-term instability in Argentina's macro economy, exchange rates fluctuated sharply, inflation rates remained high, fiscal deficit was common, and problems accumulated in the supply side. However, the legal and economic measures of the government's macro-economic management were weak, "treating the symptoms but not the disease", which resulted in widespread economic dislocation and social imbalance.

It can be said that the Washington Consensus and "shock therapy" it advocated have both failed, for the following reasons: Firstly, the efficient market is a market with full competition, orderly legal supervision and sound social credit. The Washington Consensus only focused on the competition and elevation of the basic functions of the market, that is, the market factor system and market organization system, but ignored the improvements of the basic order in the market, that is, the market legal system and market supervision system, as well as the developments and improvements of the market environment foundation (including the market environment system and market infrastructure). As a result, the market economy in the Washington Consensus was a free market economy, rather than a modern market economy with sound systems. Moreover, effective governments are governments which abide by market rules, maintain market order and participate in market competition. The Washington Consensus only recognized the guarantee of non-operational resources (social public goods) by various governments across the world, utterly ignored that governments need to "plan, guide and support" besides the responsibilities to "coordinate, supervise and manage" the competition in operational resources (industrial resources), and even neglected the necessity of governments to participate besides promoting the construction of quasi-operational resources (urban resources). Only governments that have effective policies to support the allocation of the three types of resources are strong effective governments in the mature market economy. Henceforth, the "deregulation" in the Washington Consensus was essentially anarchism, and had obvious defects compared with the theory that modern mature market economy equals strong effective government plus strong efficient market. Furthermore, for the real economic growth rate to approach or reach the potential economic growth rate, apart from improving the modern market systems, the most important task at hand is to strengthen governmental capacities, including institutional arrangements and institutional construction, transformation of development mode, etc. This was void in the Washington Consensus. To strengthen the capacities, governments not only need to abide by the rules of the market economy, but also need to control its development and take part in the competition. This requires a sound institutional environment and transformation of the mode of development. The so-called institutional environment construction includes not only improving the legislation, law enforcement and judicial systems related to the market economy, and popularizing related legal education, but also setting the subjects, contents and modes of supervision, supervising effectively the institutions, businesses, and execution of policies and regulations as the market economy requires, and establishing social and institutional norms conducive to the reform and development of government organizations. The transformation of the mode of development means that we should transform from Adam Smith's mode of "market (the invisible hand) plus focus on supply (regulation of commodity, price and supply)" or Keynes' mode of "government intervention plus focus on demand (the troika of investment, consumption and export)" to a modern mature market economic mode of "government leading (intervention) plus focus on supply (supply-side structural new engine)", that is, a "strong effective government plus strong efficient market" development mode. The government should lead foresightedly in all aspects in the entire process of market economic activities.

3 The Combination and Assessment of "Effective Government Plus Efficient Market" Mode

The relationship between governments and markets has always been one of the core disputed issues in economics, the focus being on the effects governments have on resource allocations in the market economy and their influence on economic growth, urban constructions and social livelihood.

A brief recap on the views of various economic schools as discussed above: Firstly, the mercantilism in the early stage of capitalism advocated government's intervention in economic life, prohibition of gold and silver outflows, and increases in gold and silver inflow. The main idea was that the growth of a nation's strength is based upon trade surplus, that is, when exports exceed imports, wealth can be obtained. Henceforth, it advocated that it is best if agriculture, commerce and manufacturing are regulated by governments, develop foreign trade monopoly, protect the domestic market through high tariff rates and other trade restrictions, and use the raw materials and markets from colonies for the manufacturing industry. This theory motivated the rapid development of early capitalism. Secondly, after the rise of classical economics, the market allocated the resources became the mainstream view. Adam Smith's economic liberalism and Ricardo's theory of comparative cost limited governments' functions to very small areas, their objective was merely the assurance of effective market operation. Thirdly, Keynesianism, which rose in the 1930s, advocated governmental use of expansionary economic policies to promote economic growth through increasing demand; the government should not only ensure market operation, it should also ensure supply and demand equilibrium in the economic system by interfering in the economy through monetary policies and fiscal policies. Fourthly, in the 1970s and 1980s, economists such as M. Friedman and A. B. Laffer suggested that the government should not participate in economic activities directly, etc., to solve economic crisis by improving supply, …

As we return now to the structure of six functions of the vertical modern market system, faced with the common problems in the contemporary world, namely the effective allocation of the three types of resources, we will discover that the relationship between the government and the market is not a simple relationship of two sides in a contradiction. The division of weak efficient market, semi-strong efficient market and strong efficient market is not only quantifiable, but also real history; the categorization into weak effective government, semi-strong effective government and strong effective government not only reflects the true performance of nations in market economy, but also resolves the current problem on the relationship between government and market. In theory, there exist at least nine modes for the combination of the two.

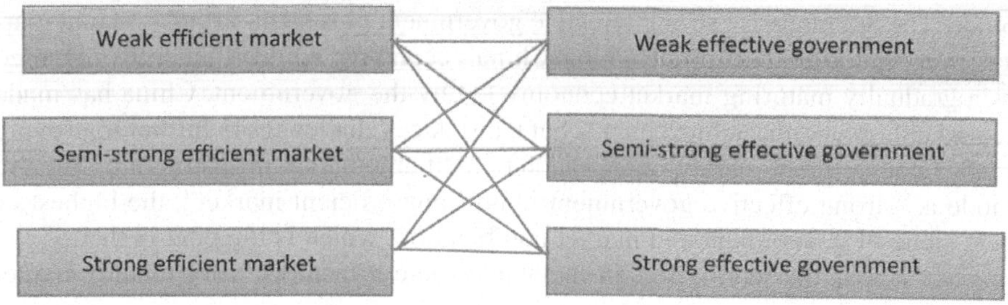

The 1st mode is "weak effective government plus weak efficient market", that is, the government does basically not regulate the economy, the market development is not complete, the market competition mechanism is often impeded, the legal system is inadequate, and disorder exists. This mode is usually prevalent in middle and low-income countries. The 2nd mode is "weak effective government plus semi-strong efficient market". Such a mode is difficult to exist in the real economy because there must be market legal system and market supervision system in semi-strong efficient markets, and it is impossible for weak effective governments to establish these systems. The 3rd mode is "weak effective government plus strong efficient market", which is purely an assumption, and there is no such case in the real world. The 4th mode is "semi-strong effective government plus weak efficient market", under which the government can better allocate non-operational resources, provide basic public goods; at the same time, the government begins to allocate and support operational resources, but is not good at grasping the market development trends, nor can it independently solve the problems arising from market operation. This situation is similar to that in 1978–1984 after China's reform and opening up, and is the operation or regulation mode in the early stages of market economy. The 5th mode is "semi-strong effective government plus semi-strong efficient market", a semi-mature market economy mode. Under this mode, on the one hand, the government can plan and guide the industrial layout, support and regulate production and operation; on the other hand, the government can continuously improve the market supervision mechanism, legal guarantee mechanism, environmental support mechanism, and others. This mode is prevalent in nations in their mid-term development stages of market economy, and is very similar to China's situation before joining the WTO. The 6th mode is "semi-strong effective government plus strong efficient market", very much in line with the current situation in the United States. During the economic development of the United States, the market plays a decisive role in the allocation of resources, whilst the government also plays an important role in the allocation of non-operational resources. However, constrained by system or ideology, the United States has been ambiguous or inconsistent when allocating operational resources and defining and developing quasi-operational resources. Hence, it has difficulties achieving a breakthrough in these two aspects, and its overall economic growth and urban upgrading are lacking in planning, not systematic nor forward-looking. The 7th mode is "strong effective government plus weak efficient market", which is difficult to exist in reality. This is because the functions of strong effective governments are at least aligning with the semi-strong efficient markets. Nations with planned economies do not belong to this mode. The 8th mode is "strong effective government plus semi-strong efficient market", very much akin to current China. China's economic mode is generally regarded as a gradually maturing market economy led by the government. China has made remarkable economic achievements, but it also faces challenges in further improving market competition, market order, market credit and market infrastructure. The 9th mode is "strong effective government plus strong efficient market", the highest or best mode of government and market combination, which is the goal in theory and practice across the world, and an inevitable route to achieve truly mature market economy.

4 Strong Effective Government Plus Strong Efficient Market Equals Mature Market Economy

As mentioned above, strong effective government essentially includes the following: firstly, it can effectively allocate non-operational resources and support them with policies, promote social harmony and stability, enhance and optimize the economic development environment; secondly, it can effectively allocate operational resources and support them with policies, maintain the openness, fairness and justice of the market, and effectively raise the overall productivity of society; thirdly, it can effectively allocate quasi-operational resources and participate in competition, promote the comprehensive and sustainable development of urban construction and socio-economy. The effectiveness of strong effective government is embodied in the integration of allocating the three types of resources, making policies and attaining the goals. There are three criteria for a strong effective government: firstly, respecting market rules; secondly, maintaining economic order and stabilizing economic development; thirdly, effectively allocating resources and participating in regional competition.

Strong efficient market essentially includes the following: firstly, the completeness of market basic functions (including market factor system and market organization system); secondly, the completeness of market basic order (including market legal system and market supervision system); and thirdly, the completeness of market environment foundation (including market environment system and market infrastructure). The efficiency of a strong efficient market is the overall effects brought about by the six subsystems of the vertical modern market system, embodied in the integration of substantial competition in production, fair market and orderly business operation. There are three criteria for a strong efficient market: firstly, substantial market competition; secondly, orderly legal supervision; and thirdly, sound social credit system.

In reality, strong effective government needs at least three conditions. Firstly, keeping pace with the times, referring mainly to the urgent need for governments to be "ahead" of new technology. Rapid development in science and technology brings new resources, new tools, new industries and new formats, which will shock the existing governmental management system. Advances in science and technology bring about new demands and higher efficiency in production and life, but at the same time, overwhelm the government with new problems. Henceforth, to function properly in economic growth, urban construction, and social livelihood, or in other words, to allocate reasonably non-operational resources, operational resources, and quasi-operational resources, the government's ideologies, policies and measures should all keep pace with the times. Secondly, all-round competition, that is, strong effective government needs to lead foresightedly, using its value, institutional, organizational, technological innovations, etc. to systematically participate in all-round competition throughout the process in all factors in social livelihood undertakings (optimizing the allocation of public goods, effectively elevating the economic development environment), economic growth (leading, supporting, regulating and supervising the market subjects, effectively increasing productivity), and urban construction development (abiding by market rules and participating in construction projects). The so-called all-round competition is based on enterprise competition, but not limited to competition in goods production in its traditional sense, but instead, encompasses the entire process of goal planning, policy making and the final outcome to achieve comprehensive and sustainable socio-economic development of the nation. Thirdly, the disclosure of government affairs, including disclosure of information on decision-making, execution, management, services, results, key items (areas), and others. The openness and transparency of government affairs can guarantee the rights of all sectors in society to know, to participate, to express, and to supervise, and better allocate resources in important areas such as economic growth, urban construction, and social livelihood. Transparent, ruled by law, innovative, service-oriented, clean and honest strong effective governments will stimulate market vitality and social creativity, and thus benefit the world and mankind.

It can be said that the relationships between governments and markets can be analogized to the "Goldbach Conjecture" in economics. The great achievements in economic growth, urban construction, social livelihood by the organic combination of effective governments and efficient markets have already been confirmed by successful cases home and abroad. Here are just three examples for illustration:

The first example is the rapid development of the Pearl River Delta, which is an epitome of the "Chinese Dream". As reported by the Russian journalist Pepe Escobar, Shenzhen in 1979 was just a barren fishing village north to Hong Kong. In the early 1990s, the Pearl River Delta just started to develop into China's largest labor-intensive manufacturing center. And today, the Pearl River Delta, with Guangzhou, Shenzhen, Foshan and Dongguan as its axis, whilst accelerating its development of high-end industries in the value chain and building first-class national manufacturing innovation centers and national science and technology industry innovation centers, is at the same time, building first-class international metropolitan clusters in its urbanization strategies. The fascination with innovation and the promotion of urbanization in the Pearl River Delta are expediting and leading China into a new socio-economic model. The Pearl River Delta in China has accomplished in just 20 years what the West spent 200 years doing. And the driving force behind the re-writing of economic development, urban construction, and social livelihood undertaking in the Pearl River

Delta is "market plus government"—the value reconstruction of an innovative market economy idea. The Pearl River Delta is continuously exploring various ways to synergize government and market, and continuously making new breakthroughs in economic growth, urban construction and social livelihood undertakings.

The second example is the "Singapore Consensus", which promotes overall social progress. In 1960, the per capita GDP of China's Hong Kong and Singapore were USD 405 and USD 428 respectively; by 1980, USD 5,700 and USD 4,927 respectively; and by 2013, USD 38,358 and USD 56,389 respectively, with Singapore far exceeding Hong Kong, China. During this period, Singapore successfully realized five economic transformations—establishing labor-intensive industries in the 1960s, establishing economic-intensive industries in the 1970s, shifting to capital-intensive industries in the 1980s, committing to technology-intensive industries in the 1990s, and focusing on knowledge-intensive industries in the 21st century. The government was the main driving force behind. The combination of government and market, and that of economic development policies and social development policies, effectively stroke a balance between efficiency and fairness, development and stability, and promoted economic growth, urban upgrading and overall social progress. What the world has commended as the "Singapore Consensus", was precisely the fruit of "effective government plus efficient market", and is leading the nation to comprehensive and sustainable developments.

The third example is the world-class urban clusters established in the Great Bay Area of Guangdong, Hong Kong and Macao. Speaking of great bay areas, people naturally think of the Tokyo Bay Area, the San Francisco Bay Area and the New York Bay Area. These three bay areas connecting the coastline are all core economic and cultural urban clusters of their nations. The Tokyo Bay Area has the headquarters of Toyota, Sony, Mitsubishi, and other Fortune Global 500 companies; the San Francisco Bay Area has Apple, Google, Facebook, and other Internet giants; whilst the New York Bay Area has gathered a large number of financial institutions there, becoming the heartland of global finance. The Great Bay Area of Guangdong, Hong Kong and Macao refers to the nine cities that constitute the Pearl River Delta Economic Zone, including Guangzhou, Shenzhen, Zhuhai, Dongguan, Huizhou, Zhongshan, Foshan, Zhaoqing and Jiangmen, as well as the two special administrative regions of Hong Kong and Macao. The construction of the urban clusters in the Great Bay Area of Guangdong, Hong Kong and Macao, shall set those of Tokyo and New York as a benchmark, and surpass them. In 2016, the GDP of the Guangdong, Hong Kong and Macao Great Bay Area was about USD 1.38 trillion, comparable to that of the ROK, which ranked 11th in the world economy. The ports handling capacity reached 65.2 million TEU (Twenty-foot Equivalent Unit), exceeding the sum of the Tokyo, New York and San Francisco Bay Areas. The passenger throughput at the airports reached 186 million, ranking the highest amongst the bay areas. In 2016, the total value of imports and exports in the Guangdong, Hong Kong and Macao Great Bay Area reached USD 1,796.67 billion, received foreign direct investment USD 102.91 billion, accounting for 5.9% of global FDI inflows. In 2017, China's "Government Work Report" emphasized promoting the construction of the Guangdong, Hong Kong and Macao Great Bay Area, striving to make it a first-class international bay area and world-class urban cluster.

Specific measures include:

(1) Promoting infrastructure interconnectivity and building world-class urban clusters, that is, accelerating the coordinated development of Bay Area ports, airports and rapid transportation networks, and actively constructing infrastructure of the import and export ports;
(2) Accelerating the development of logistics and shipping and establishing world-class shipping clusters, which includes accelerating the construction of free trade ports, vigorously developing the intermodal logistics system, upgrading the Bay Area shipping services, and others;
(3) Promoting scientific and technological innovation, resource sharing and building an international center for scientific and technological innovation: Apart from constructing infrastructure for science and technology in the Bay Area, establishing science and technology transfer mechanism, encouraging the youths to innovate and start their own businesses, and promoting the development of finance for science and technology, there are also needs to outsource services for science and technology and protect intellectual property cooperatively;
(4) Promoting integrated developments of manufacturing industries and building a "Made in China 2025" demonstration zone, which will promote the coordinated development of manufacturing industrial chains, strengthen industrial informatization, promote international cooperation in production capacity, and encourage the equipment manufacturing industry to enter the international market;
(5) Enhancing innovative developments of the financial industry and establishing an international hub, which includes strengthening finances in shipping, actively innovating finances in science and technology, promoting the integration of industry and finance, accelerating the construction of financial platforms, and promoting the docking of offshore finance and onshore finance;
(6) Strengthening integration in the Bay Area, and creating a circle of quality life suitable for living, business and tourism: The rise of the Guangdong, Hong Kong and Macao Great Bay Area has created a new development pattern, and become the new engine for regional economy, and all these are attributed to the dual function of "effective government plus efficient market". It is in the framework of this strategic planning that the Guangdong, Hong Kong and Macao Great Bay Area has achieved substantial developments.

Chapter 9
Building Up a New Engine for Global Economic Development

1 Kindleberger Trap and Endogenous Growth Theory

In order to discuss the building of a new engine for global economic development, it is necessary to review two economic theories, the Kindleberger Trap and Endogenous Growth Theory.

As Joseph S. Nye, a well-known US political scientist and professor at Harvard University, wrote in January 2017 in his article "The Kindleberger Trap", "Charles Kindleberger, an intellectual architect of the Marshall Plan who later taught at MIT, argued that the disastrous decade of the 1930s was caused when the US replaced Britain as the largest global power but failed to take on Britain's role in providing global public goods. The result was the collapse of the global system into depression, genocide, and world war."

Professor Nye pointed out, "Small countries have little incentive to pay for such global public goods. Because their small contributions make little difference to whether they benefit or not, it is rational for them to ride for free. But the largest powers can see the effect and feel the benefit of their contributions. So it is rational for the largest countries to lead. When they do not, global public goods are under-produced." In his view, Donald Trump, the President-elect of the United States, should heed lessons drawn from others' mistakes when formulating his policies toward China: the Thucydides Trap that if an established power (such as the United States) becomes too fearful of a rising country (such as China), war will become unavoidable, as well as the Kindleberger Trap—a China that seems too weak rather than too strong.[1]

Nevertheless, if we meticulously examine the situation, China has played a fairly constructive role in the global governance system and has achieved developments in stages from capital supply to institutional construction and then to value innovation. Since 2008, China has begun contributing more capital to global governance, including injecting capital to promote multilateralization of the "Chiang Mai Initiative", to

Y. Chen, *New Economic Engine: Effective Government and Efficient Market*, China Academic Library, https://doi.org/10.1007/978-981-15-2922-1_9

the International Monetary Fund and the World Bank. Moreover, China has been taking part in global governance with regard to institutional construction. As landmarks, China launched the "Belt and Road" Initiative and started the Asian Infrastructure Investment Bank in 2013, and in 2014, China put forward the construction of the New Development Bank of BRICs. And since 2016, starting from the Hangzhou Summit of the G20 in particular, China has begun contributing ideas and philosophies to global governance. From capital to institutions and then to philosophies, China is gradually becoming a mature and responsible leading country.

In Kindleberger's view, global public goods included the international trade system, the international monetary system, capital flows, macroeconomic policies and crisis management mechanisms, etc. Joseph E. Stiglitz, Nobel Laureate in Economics and professor at Columbia University, believed on the other hand, that global public goods included five major categories, namely international economic stability, international security, international environment, international humanitarian assistance and knowledge.

At this point, putting aside the political and ideological disputes brought about by the Kindleberger's Trap for the time being, merely from the perspective of economics, there are at least three problems to be solved: Firstly, what are the global public goods? Or in other words, what kind of products can be regarded as global public goods? Secondly, who will provide the global public goods? Thirdly, how are such global public goods to be provided or accepted?

Let's put aside the above-mentioned questions and turn to the Endogenous Growth Theory for a while. Endogenous Growth Theory is a branch of macroeconomic theories that originated in the mid-1980s. Its core idea is that the economy can grow sustainably without relying on external forces, endogenous technological progress being the decisive factor of sustained economic growth. This theory emphasizes incomplete competition and progressive increases in returns.

Since the era of Adam Smith, the debate throughout the entire circle of economics has revolved around the factors driving economic growth for more than 200 years. The eventual consensus is that, for a long period of time, the economic growth of a nation mainly depends on the following three factors. Firstly, the accumulation of productive resources over time; secondly, the utilization efficiency of resource stock with a nation's given technological knowledge; and thirdly, technological progress. However, the most popular neoclassical economic growth theory since the 1960s takes technological progress as an exogenous factor for economic growth, and concludes that long-term economic growth will stop when factor income diminishes. On the other hand, the newly-formed endogenous growth theory in the 1990s holds that the long-term growth rate is dependent on endogenous factors. In other words, the process of labor input includes human capital arising from formal education, training, and on-the-job training; and the process of accumulating material capital includes technological progress arising from R&D, innovation and other activities. Henceforth, this theory internalizes technological progress and other factors, and concludes that due to the technological progress, factor income will progressively increase, thereby long-term growth rate is positive. As a result, the orientation of policies of neoclassical economic growth theory and that of endogenous growth theory differ from each other.

As theories develop, many economists realize that the biggest problem faced by endogenous growth theory is how to conduct empirical analysis. This empirical research is, in fact, to be carried out along two technical routes: one is on differences amongst nations to find evidence of endogenous growth; the other is on economic growth factors based on a nation's long-term data, or on a specific factor independently, such as the effects of opening up policies, taxation, equality, financial progress, education expenditure, innovation and other factors on economic growth.

At this point, I have no intention to introduce too more about the relevant models of endogenous growth theory and its modern development, and the revival of the so-called Neo-Schumpeterism. I just want to reiterate that the traditional economists who study a nation's economic growth factors are at this stage, still confined to the industrial economy as described by Adam Smith, still looking for new driving forces for growth therein, and still believing that technological progress is the deciding factor in endogenous growth.

I do not judge endogenous growth theory. I just want to point out that: (1) The endogenous growth of an economy refers to the sustainable development of a nation's economy. (2) The discussion on endogenous economic growth factors should not always be confined to industrial economy, but should encompass the three economic fields, namely, industrial economy, livelihood economy and urban economy. (3) I do not object to traditional economists looking for impetus in endogenous growth (such as technology, etc.) from the scarcity of resources in industrial economy, but at this stage, we should look more from the resource generation in urban economy. (4) The newly generated resources in the three types of resources, which is mainly, at this moment, the urban economy with investment and construction of the software and hardware infrastructure and even the development and operation of intelligent cities as its main contents, followed by economies in emerging areas of space, deep sea, polar resources and network, are not only social quasi-public goods, but also global quasi-public goods, and even a new economic growth pole or in other words, the new engine for global economic development.

Take international aid, a global public good as an example. It is interrelated with the three types of resources and the three types of economy, and can be divided into social-typed, economic-typed, and environmental-typed. International aid that is associated with the livelihood economy across the world is public welfare-like, and can be called social-typed international aid. International aid that is associated with the industrial economy across the world is commodity-like, and can be called economic-typed international aid. International aid that is associated with the urban economy across the world can be called environmental-typed international aid. International disaster relief, relief, poverty alleviation, medical treatment, education and others are supplied to the international community for free through the United Nations and other organizations, and are therefore public welfare-like and social-typed. The related products from the three major industries are commodity-like, and are supplied to the international community through import and export and related institutions, under the guidance of market rules, which is economic-typed international aid. The investment and construction of infrastructure software and hardware between nations, which are aid or business in nature, or both, are environmental-typed international aid. The type to be adopted is determined by the relationship between nations and many other factors.

Thus far, we have discussed the classification and characterization of the three types of resources, the three types of economy and the corresponding government policies, and the classification, characterization and supply of international aid; and this effectively solves the problems of what global public goods are, where they are coming from and going to in the Kindleberger Trap. The newly generated resources based on infrastructure investment and construction are not only globalized quasi-public goods, but also a new engine for national or even global economic development.

2 The Arrival of the Era of Urbanization-Led Economic Growth

There are competitions among countries and cities across the world, including China. Cities are major participants in global competition, the yardstick to measure innovation of major nations, and the window to decode the interactions between markets and governments. Foshan City, Guangdong Province, where I served as Secretary of the CPC Municipal Committee and Mayor, is taking Chengdu, Wuhan, Hangzhou, Nanjing, Qingdao, Changsha, Wuxi, Ningbo, Dalian, Zhengzhou and other domestic cities with similar economic aggregates as benchmarks. These cities are benchmarks for one another, striving to build a "sample pool" of urban innovation, and exploring for sustainable urban economic growth.

Referring to the effective measures taken by other big cities, Foshan has made many plans and arrangements. (1) Being three major manufacturing cities, Wuxi, Ningbo and Foshan should adhere to the real economy and focus on intelligent manufacturing. Foshan, in particular, needs to speed up "Made in China 2025". (2) Drawing on the experience of cultivating new industrial clusters in Chengdu, Wuhan and Nanjing, Foshan should cultivate new economic growth poles in intelligent equipment, new energy vehicles and other fields. (3) Backed by Guangzhou, the "mega city", Foshan needs to link with it to provide intra-city services. (4) Foshan should compete in attracting business, to attract the Fortune Global 500 enterprises. (5) Foshan should innovate financially to dedicatedly serve the real economy. (6) Foshan should take urbanization, industrial and urban integration as the new pivot for urban competition. (7) Regional competition and cooperation has entered the "urban cluster era". Referring to the experience of Wuhan's and Chengdu's building of hub cities—expediting the construction of major transport hubs, Foshan should build three-dimensional transportation and make every effort to promote a new round of infrastructure construction. (8) Foshan should hasten the construction of an intelligent city, to establish a new service system conducive to living, business and tourism and find the new "key" to stimulate urban economic growth.

Following Foshan's example, Beijing-Tianjin-Hebei, the Pearl River Delta and Yangtze River Delta, being China's three major economic growth poles, are all fully implementing urban and rural planning, promoting infrastructure construction, planning industrial layout, protecting environment, and improving the level of public services, to promote regional integration and sustainable development of regional economy. These measures have had remarkable results. At present, the infrastructure integration of the three economic circles are progressing orderly, the level of labor division and cooperation advanced among regions, newly styled urbanization steadily promoted, and national sponge cities and national utility tunnels constructed orderly. At the same time, other regional urban clusters in China have taken many significant measures with remarkable results in their continuous promotion of regional coordinated developments and cultivation of new economic growth poles.

In addition to regional governments' diligent efforts, the central government has also made great efforts to promote investment and construction of such basic fields as big science projects, national science and technology major projects, and major science and technology platforms. At the same time, the interconnected rural transport infrastructure network is also forming an orderly new structure, and promoting the urban-rural integration. Infrastructure constructions of transportation, municipal administration, energy, water conservancy, information, environmental protection and others are precisely laying solid foundations for cultivating new economic growth points, and will continuously produce massive economic and social effects.

The era of urbanization-led economic growth has arrived. As far as China was concerned, 2013 was a turning point especially, when the situation of "excessive industrialization and backward urbanization" that mainly depends on industrial economy has begun to change, urbanization has become a new momentum for economic growth, and in turn gradually promoted the transformation and upgrading of industrial economy.

3 Community of National Interests

From a worldwide perspective, the global population has been gathering in major cities in the recent more than half a century. The scale of cities and economic efficiency, per capita urban output and urban population size are significantly positively correlated. The larger the scale of cities, the higher the productivity. The United States, Japan, ROK, Singapore, Australia, and Canada, etc., are as such; their economic activities are concentrated in large metropolitan areas, where the economic output of large cities is far greater.

From the perspective of urban development, PPP (public private partnership) is an effective method to integrate government and market. Darrin Grimsey and Mervyn K. Lewis suggested in the book *Public Private Partnership: The Worldwide Revolution in Infrastructure Provision and Project Finance* that the greatest advantage of the PPP method lies in introducing market mechanism into infrastructure investment and financing. Its specific effects include: (1) introducing competition mechanism to promote building government integrity; (2) alleviating the shortage of funds due to the government's lack of money, and accelerating the construction of infrastructure and development of public utilities; (3) giving full play to the initiatives and creativities of foreign and private enterprises, and improving the efficiency in project operation and the quality of services; (4) effectively promoting the completeness of market laws and regulations; (5) promoting technology transfer; (6) training professionals and experts; (7) promoting the development of financial markets; (8) reducing capital expenditures for foreign and private enterprises, and achieving "big projects from small investments"; (9) alleviating the debt burden of investors through off-balance-sheet financing; (10) making use of the limited recourse to allocate risks rationally, strengthen the control of project income, and maintain a high rate of return on investment (compared to full recourse).

In addition, during the process of building the "Belt and Road", China will develop the Industrial Parks represented by the "Silk Road Post Stations" into the major platform to support economy and trade interconnections and industrial development. We will start from constructing core traffic nodes such as seaports, airports and inland waterless ports, and take the Industrial Parks neighboring these ports as the core and main carriers to systematically solve the problems restricting the industrial transfer of host nations caused by weaknesses in the software and hardware. This way China will summarize an effective development mode of PPC (Port Park City). The core of this mode is the development, construction and operation of ports. Through advance management followed by Industrial Parks and development of supporting urban functions, host nations will achieve regional interconnected developments, forming a relatively complete ecological circle of ports, logistics and financial parks. PPC has become a new business card for the circulation of trade and interconnection construction of nations along the "Belt and Road"; international economic cooperation characterized by "infrastructure construction and supporting Industrial Parks" has also become a new mode for international economic growth.

The infrastructure construction is becoming more and more important in economic development. In 2016, KPMG International put forward ten major trends that would change the world of infrastructure over the next five years in the world economic development: (1) The macro risk environment has begun to shift. (2) Competition for investment heats up. (3) The investment interest is focusing on the larger benefits to unclog the pipeline. (4) The asset management gets more sophisticated. (5) Technology rockets up the infrastructure agenda. (6) Security has become an important issue in urban construction. (7) The gap between public and private narrows. (8) Through financial innovations, institutions will promote the rapid rise in the investment of infrastructure constructions. (9) The institutional debt market takes off. (10) China and India have been making a leap. KPMG's report was an observation and judgment of global infrastructure construction, revealing the possible route of world economic growth.

"Research Report on Economic Focus of G20 (2016–2017)" also demonstrated the importance of infrastructure constructions, holding that the prominent highlight in the economic operation of the Group of 20 is the investment and construction of infrastructure, which is an important engine driving the recovery of the world economy and its sustainable growth. As the report pointed out: (1) The supply of infrastructure in emerging and developing economics is obviously inadequate with a huge gap, whilst the existing infrastructure in developed economies are gradually aging; hence there is a great demand for infrastructure construction across the world. (2) During a period of global economic downturn and investment inefficiency, strengthening investments in infrastructure, especially promoting and optimizing high-quality investments, will strongly motivate economic growth in the short and long term, and will also create employment and improve productivity. (3) Being a part of the new growth strategy, increasing investments in infrastructure is also the common focus of the G20 and a key issue in the G20 Summit. The G20 Summit held in November 2014 agreed to establish a Global Infrastructure Hub with a four-year mandate, which aims to develop "a knowledge-sharing platform and network between governments, the private sector, development banks and other international organizations. The Hub will foster collaboration among these groups to improve the functioning and financing of infrastructure markets." (4) In October 2014, the World Bank launched Global Infrastructure Facility (GIF) to deliver complex public-private infrastructure projects and encourage more private infrastructure investment. (5) In recent years, the BRICS economic cooperation and regional economic cooperation in Asia have also attached great importance to joint infrastructure constructions with such fruitful collaboration as the BRICS New Development Bank and Asian Infrastructure Investment Bank. (6) According to the estimate of the Global Infrastructure Hub, there will be an investment gap of USD10 trillion to USD20 trillion in the infrastructure investment market by 2030, which will adversely affect the global economic development. Therefore, in 2016, the Global Infrastructure Hub called on governments across the world to re-focus on infrastructure investment, exploit development opportunities with great investment potential, and boost the global economy, etc. As can be predicted, with the profound development of regional or global economic integration, the demand for cross-regional and cross-border interconnected infrastructure will increase day by day, while the global infrastructure construction is ushering in a new round of development opportunities. The rapid growth of infrastructure investments will be an important engine driving the recovery of the world economy and its sustainable growth.[2]

In the 5th chapter of this book, we have analyzed the scale effects, cluster effects and neighborhood effects of urban economic development, which is mainly based on the investment and development of the software and hardware infrastructure, and even on the development and operation of intelligent cities. As the economic growth across the world enters a new stage of urbanization and urban-rural integration, the investment and construction of global infrastructure has condensed all nations into a community of interests. All nations need to invest resources, coordinate with each other, formulate rules and promote accordingly in order to maximize the due important role of the new engine for world economic growth.

4 Building Up a New Engine for Global Economic Development

In 1948, Ragnar Nurkse likened trade to the growth engine of the 19th century to justify the strategy of substituting imports for industrialization. During the financial crisis in 2012–2014, the annual growth rate of global trade was less than 4%, which was far below the average growth rate of about 7% before the crisis. Consequently, World Bank officials once again raised the question on how to "restart" the global trade engine. I believe that the world economy generally develops from the factor-driven stage to the investment-driven stage, and then to the innovation-driven stage. Many nations, especially those rich in natural resources such as oil, natural gas, minerals and agricultural products, etc., whose economic growth was driven by tangible factors like land and labor force, have reached their extremes with signs of unsustainability.

Henceforth, a new engine is needed to realize economic growth in the new century. In my opinion, in the modern market system made up of "effective government plus efficient market", a new structural engine on the supply side (rather than a "trade engine" on the demand side) will give full play in competition to enterprises in the allocation of industrial resources and to the government in that of urban resources. These new structural engines on the supply side include investment engines, innovation engines and regulation engines that combine tangible and intangible factors, and will have important effects on global economic governance and development.

Building Up a New Engine for Global Investment

Investment-driven growth depends not only on the supply-side allocation and competition of products and industrial resources, but also on the supply-side competitive performance of the government in allocating urban resources and promoting infrastructure construction. It can bring about capital growth to nations, promote technological innovation and deepen market mechanisms' development, as well as increase employment, thereby it has long-term sustainability. In order to build a new engine for global investment, we should take the following measures:

First, to promote the structural reform in the supply side, which includes the following two aspects:

Firstly, promoting new industrialization that is driven by and in turn advances informatization: The new industrialization fully exploits science and technology as well as advantages of human resources with better economic benefits and little environmental pollution by consuming less resources. It encompasses three aspects: (1) Supporting and guiding the transformation and upgrading of traditional industries—Scientific and technological progress can be used to transform those old industries which consume resources and the environment into new recycling industries. Technological transformation can revitalize huge stock assets, optimize and enhance industrial efficiency, stimulate demand, and promote economic growth. (2) Supporting and cultivating strategic emerging industries and high-tech industries—On the foundation of the information industry, intelligent industries, which are incremental assets, should be developed across the world. Intelligent industry is a new industrial structure with human intelligence, computer network and physical equipment as basic elements, and its growth is of a green development mode. Nations should focus on supporting and nurturing R&D innovation, achievement transformation and industrialization of core and key technologies of enterprises, cultivate dominant industries and leading industries, and build a sound industrial chain and modern service network. (3) With the help of market competition, nations should promote mergers and acquisitions, integration and reorganization of enterprises, eliminate old industries constantly, promote the development of new industries, usher industrialization to a higher level, and enhance the core competitiveness of enterprises. This is one of the important means to realize the effective investment and transfer between new and old forces on the supply side.

Secondly, expediting the modernization of agriculture: It refers to the process and means by which traditional agriculture transforms to modern agriculture. During this process, agriculture has increasingly had at its disposal, modern industries, modern scientific technology and modern economic management techniques. Nations should utilize modern development ideas to combine agricultural development with the building of an ecological civilization and transform the outdated traditional agriculture into eco-agriculture with the advanced productivity of the contemporary world. Specifically, agricultural modernization includes not only the expansion of land management, but also the "modernization of farmers". Nations should guide farmers to overcome ignorance and backwardness and become "educated, skilled and capable" modern farmers. In terms of organizational mode, whether large or small-scale family-run farms, nations should support farmers' cooperative organizations or assist in dispersing farmers to cater to the market, so that they can provide one-stop services in pre-production, mid-production and post-production process, as well as a one-stop operation process from the purchase of the means of production, to storage, processing, transportation, and sales of agricultural products. In addition, nations should promote operations in an appropriate scale, appropriate urbanization, and vocational education in agricultural technology. In a word, agricultural modernization includes advanced production means, scientific production technology, industrialized operation, socialized agricultural services, regional industrial layout, and the overall modernization of agricultural infrastructure, ecological environment, competency of agricultural laborers and farmers' lives. The modernization of agriculture can create a stable social environment for industrialization and urbanization, reduce social costs and prosper the economies across the world.

Second, to increase investments and construction of infrastructure, which includes three aspects:

Firstly, promoting new urbanization—The urbanization is characterized by overall coordinated urban and rural planning, urban and rural integration, industrial interaction, frugality and intensity, ecological livability and harmonious development. It is where large, medium-sized and small cities, small towns, and new rural communities mutually promote and develop coordinately. In developed nations, the urban population generally accounts for more than 80%. As the urban-rural integration accelerates and the city-centered urban pattern are formed across the world, planning and constructing new human-oriented towns, constructing facilities for basic urban public services such as education, medical treatment, culture, sports and others, as well as developing recreational tourism, business logistics, information industry, transportation and others, will provide new growth potential to the world.

Secondly, promoting the modernization of infrastructure—This includes the modernization of energy, transportation, environmental protection, information, irrigation and others. For example, promoting comprehensive urban transportation construction, building convenient regional transportation network; speeding up the construction of sponge cities to enhance the ability of urban disaster prevention and mitigation; building and improving the drainage and waterlogging prevention system to effectively eliminate the risk of urban waterlogging; promoting the treatment of urban black and odious water bodies, to improve the quality of the urban water resource environment; improving regional parkland to share a common green life; building urban utility tunnel for pipelines to operate orderly and efficiently; strengthening urban water supply facilities to guarantee the water supply security; optimizing orderly the urban energy supply to vigorously promote urban energy conservation and emission reduction; enhancing the efficiency of waste and sewage facilities to achieve resource conservation and recycling; enhancing the construction of information infrastructure to promote the development of intelligent cities; etc. The investment in this area has great room and potential, which can effectively promote economic growth across the world.

Moreover, promoting the development and construction of intelligent cities—An intelligent city is a system, also known as a network city, digital city or information city. It is built upon human brain wisdom, computer network, physical equipment and other basic factors, which form intelligent urban management. It includes intelligent infrastructure like intelligent transportation, intelligent electric power, intelligent buildings, intelligent environmental protection, intelligent security; intelligent social life like intelligent medical treatment, intelligent education, and intelligent families; as well as intelligent social productions like intelligent enterprises, intelligent banks, and intelligent stores. Intelligent urban systems can comprehensively raise the modernization level of urban production, life, management and operation, and further open up a new route for economic growth across the world.

Third, to increase the investment in scientific and technological projects, such as the NNMI of the US, which invested USD 1 billion in the first phase and set up 45 manufacturing innovation institutes within 10 years; as well as "Knowledge Transfer Partnership" of the UK, and the Industry 4.0 for intelligent manufacturing based on CPS (Cyber-Physics System) of Germany. These measures can integrate the innovative resources of talents, enterprises and social institutions, guide the directions for industrial R&D, and promote industrial upgrading and development. Investments across the world in big data, cloud computing, the Internet of Things, NBIC (nanotechnology, biotechnology, information technology, cognitive science) and others, will upgrade economies across the world sustainably.

Fourth, to enhance financial support capacities: Nations not only need supporting policies to guide the financial industry to serve the real economy, but also need to promote the integration of finance, science and technology, and industries through the innovation of policies. The reform, innovation and development of the financial system are indispensable for investment in the new economic engine.

Building Up a New Engine for Global Innovation

For a region, a nation, or even the world, as they enter a transitional period of economic development mode, the economic form develops from industrial resources allocation through enterprise competition to urban resources allocation through government competition, and the engine of economic growth develops from a single market mechanism to an "effective government plus efficient market" mechanism. These new circumstances in global economic development would inevitably lead to a series of new problems, such as how to maintain the principles of fairness and justice in the global economic governance system, how to protect the interests of developing nations in the global economic order, how to maintain or enhance the degree of openness of the economic system in order to resist protectionism, and how to formulate norms to face challenges in new economic fields (such as the network). In order to combat these challenges, the existing public mechanisms or public goods (including ideological, material, organizational and institutional public goods) that coordinate and govern the global economic order need to be innovated and improved.

Firstly, we should promote the innovations of value public goods, that is, ideas. To begin with, the market should be an efficient market. The vertical modern market system is a complete system composed of six subsystems. Some nations overemphasized the competition between market factors and market organizations, while neglecting the construction of the legal supervision system and the perfection of the market environment system and market infrastructure, which will deviate from the market principles of openness, fairness and justice. Moreover, the government should be an effective government. Governments across the world should not only plan, guide, support, coordinate, supervise and manage the allocation of operational resources, that is, industrial resources; but also ensure general underpinning and guarantee fairness and justice, and effectively upgrade non-operational resources, that is, social public goods. They should also adjust and compete in the allocation of quasi-operational resources, that is, urban resources. Furthermore, the mature market economic mode pursued across the world should be "strong effective government plus strong efficient market"; in the macro system of market economy, industrial resources should be allocated through enterprise competition, and urban resources through government competition. Governments across the world should play an important role in global economic growth.

Secondly, we should promote the innovations of material public goods, that is, technology. The most typical path for current developments in science and technology is the integration of informatization and industrialization, urbanization and agricultural modernization, to promote the modernization of infrastructure, which in Chinese, is termed "Internet+". Through building intelligent cities which combine tangible and intangible factors, governments provide intelligent public transport, urban management, education, medical treatment, cultural, commercial, government administration, environmental protection, energy and public security services to the society; and create a safe, efficient, convenient, green and harmonious development environment for the social economy and livelihood undertakings. These not only benefit people, but also accelerate industrialization transformation, urbanization and internationalization of cities and even nations, thus further promote the rise of emerging nations.

Thirdly, we should promote the innovations of organizational public goods, that is, management. As far as organizational management is concerned, there are similarities between that of a city, and that of a nation or even the world. Traditional urban construction and organizational frameworks, such as "urban sprawl", are prone to traffic lights failure, road congestion, traffic jam, air pollution, inefficiency, and other problems even if there are first, second, third, fourth, and even fifth ring roads. The development of modern cities requires grouped-layouts planned scientifically. Just as network development will reshape the spatial order and global supply chain development will "erase national boundaries", group-based urban development structure can effectively solve the series of problems brought about by traditional urban sprawl. Similar to the urban structure, the organization and management of the world economic order needs to reform from the urban sprawl mode towards the grouped-layout, and continuously innovate and develop; however, this requires corresponding new rules and necessary "infrastructure" investment, so that a rational layout can be formed to promote harmonious and sustainable development of the world.

Fourthly, we should promote the innovations of institutional public goods, that is, rules. The construction of a nation is guided by the triad of conceptual planning, urban and rural planning and land use planning. Within this framework, the specific policies on strategic planning, layout positioning, implementation criteria, policy evaluation, legal protection and others are systematically formulated with multiple layers. Global economic governance is framed by the Charter of the United Nations and the regulatory mechanisms of UNCTAD, the OECD and WTO. Nations around the world strive towards "making globalization bring more opportunities" and "sharing the fruits of economic growth in an all-inclusive manner". The importance of rules in global economic development is evident here. Faced with the current new circumstances, we should innovate thoughts on economic growth and relevant institutional rules, promote the structural reform of fiscal and monetary policies across the world, and maintain the consistency and coordination of economy, labor, employment and social policies. Only with equal emphasis on demand management and supply-side reform, combination of short-term policies with medium-term and long-term policies, common progress of social economic development and environmental protection, and mutual consultation, establishment and sharing of the global economic governance layout, can the global economy achieve healthy and sustainable growth.

Building Up a New Engine for Global Rules

To build a "Four I's" world economy that is innovative, invigorative, interconnected and inclusive, improvements in the global economic governance system are needed. Corresponding to non-operational resources across the world are the international public goods supply systems; corresponding to operational resources across the world are the international industrial resources allocation systems; and corresponding to quasi-operational resources are the global urban resources allocation systems. They each operate in adherence to the rules which exist objectively. A sound global economic governance system requires corresponding international rules, as follows:

Firstly, the rules on international security order—peace and stability: This is a consensus across the world and the basic guarantee of the international public goods supply system. Nations across the world should strive together to strengthen international security cooperation, protect the purposes and principles of the Charter of the United Nations, maintain the basic criteria for international relations, create a peaceful, stable, just and reasonable international security order, and build a healthy and orderly environment for economic development.

Secondly, the rules on international economic competition—fairness and efficiency: This is the basic criterion for enterprise competition in the industrial resources allocation systems across the world. As an example, the G20 formulated the guiding principles of "promoting trade and investment openness", including reducing tariff and non-tariff barriers to trade, reducing barriers to and restrictions on foreign direct investment, implementing trade facilitation measures to reduce cross-border transaction costs, appropriately reducing border restrictions on trade and investment, promoting broader cross-border coordination, and minimizing discriminatory measures against the third party through multilateral, plurilateral and bilateral agreements, etc. As another example, the guiding principles of "promoting competition and improving the business environment", including strengthening and implementing competition law, reducing administrative and legal barriers for starting enterprises and expanding operations, promoting fair market competition, implementing efficient bankruptcy proceedings, reducing restrictive provisions that hinder competition, reducing additional burdens on regulatory compliance, as well as effectively supervising regulatory policies, strengthening the rule of law, improving judicial efficiency, combating corruption, etc. All these are the rules on fairness and efficiency that need to be adhered to when nations guiding and standardizing enterprise competition across the world.

Thirdly, the rules on international common governance—cooperation and win-win situations: This is the basic criterion that must be adhered to by intergovernmental competitions in the urban resources allocation systems. Both tangible and intangible factors exist in urban resources. Amongst these, new urbanization, intelligent city development, and investments in the modernization of infrastructure with energy, transportation, environmental protection, information and water conservancy as the subjects, will be the new engine for economic growth across the world, which can bring about capital expansion, increase in employment, technological innovation, deepening of market, sustainable economic growth, social benefits, environmental improvements, enhancing of national strength and other effects. Due to differences in their pace of urbanization, policies and institutional arrangements, effects and competitiveness of investment-driven growth are different in different nations. However, the competitions between governments should be cooperative and sustainable so as to jointly enhance the global economic governance system and innovate the economic growth mode. The basic principle should be win-win cooperation. Building up an innovative, invigorative, interconnected and inclusive world economic system with win-win cooperation as its core, will promote sustained innovation in the growth mode, enhance the level of global economic governance, and thus benefiting various nations and the world.

Notes

1. Joseph S. Nye. "The Kindleberger Trap", Project Syndicate, Jan. 9, 2017, https://www.project-syndicate.org/commentary/trump-china-kindleberger-trap-by-joseph-s--nye-2017-01?barrier=accesspaylog.
2. Li Jianping, et al. eds. *Research Report on Economic Focuses of G20 (2016–2017)*. Beijing: Economic Science Press, 2016, pp. 39–42.

Appendix On Microeconomics, Mezzoeconomics, and Macroeconomics

The traditional economics system is classified into microeconomics and macroeconomics. In my opinion though, the modern economics system should be classified into three branches: microeconomics, mezzo-economics and macroeconomics. They are complementary, each with different focuses, forming a whole that manifests the roles, functions and codes of conduct of enterprises, regional governments and nations (including international economic governance organizations) with respect to resource allocations in the market economy.

A.1 Microeconomics

Microeconomics, as a branch of modern economics, regards single economic units (single producers, single consumers, single economic activities in the market) as its subject of research.

The fundamental problem in microeconomic research is how to allocate industrial resources. Its basic theory is that supply and demand determine the relative price. Its core idea is that free exchange tends to maximize the utilization of resources, under which case the allocation of resources is considered to be Pareto Optimality. Thus, the main areas of microeconomics encompass consumer choice, firm supply and income distribution, with the price theory as its core; hence, microeconomics, under many circumstances, is also called "price theory and its applications".

Microeconomics, which studies the economic behavior of individuals in the market and the corresponding economic variables, sets off from the scarcity of industrial resources and deems it the code of conduct for individuals to capitalize on the limited resources to the greatest possible extent so as to obtain maximum benefits and examine accordingly the conditions under which individuals maximize their benefits. The codes of conduct in commodity and labor markets are as follows: (1) Consumers choose commodities according to their prices to obtain the maximum

Y. Chen, *New Economic Engine: Effective Government and Efficient Market*, China Academic Library, https://doi.org/10.1007/978-981-15-2922-1

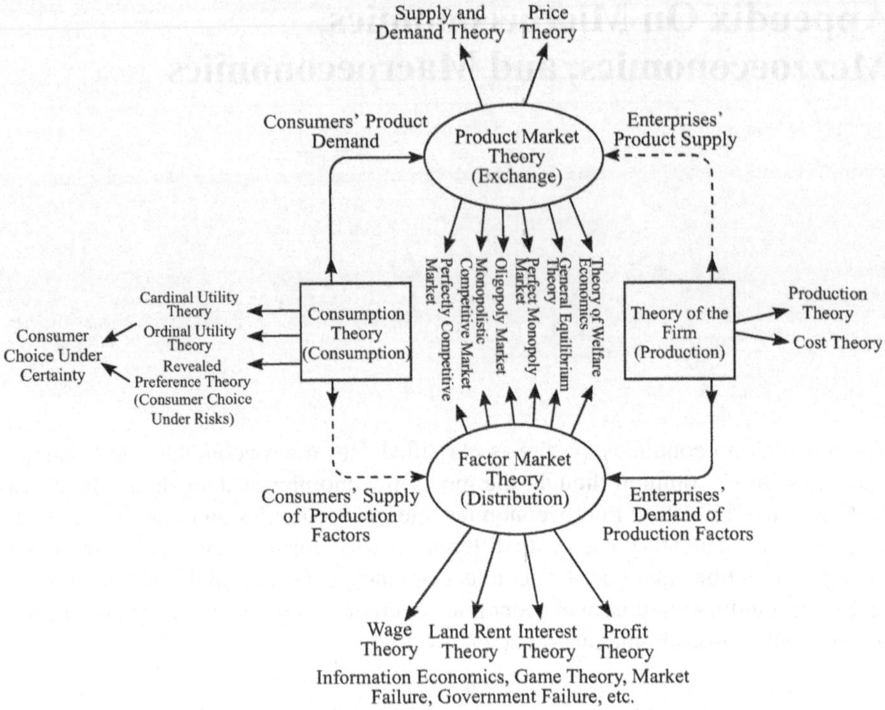

Fig. A.1 Microeconomics Theory System

utility or satisfaction from the commodities purchased with their limited income. (2) Manufacturers are the suppliers of goods and services, aiming to use minimum costs to produce the most output and obtain maximum profits. (3) The choices made by consumers and manufacturers are manifested through the supply and demand in the market and affect prices, the changes of which, in turn, coordinate the supply and demand. It follows, therefore, that the effects of market mechanisms, the attainment of equilibrium prices, the optimal allocation of industrial resources, the failure of market mechanisms, the government intervention and others, are the main contents of microeconomic research.

The history of microeconomics can be traced back to Adam Smith's *Wealth of Nations* and Alfred Marshall's *Principles of Economics*. After the 1930s, the British economist Joan Robinson and the American economist Edward Hastings Chamberlin proposed the theory of equilibrium of the firm on the basis of Marshall's theory of equilibrium price. The proposals of the equilibrium price theory, the consumer behavior theory, the producer behavior theory, the equilibrium theory of the firm, welfare economics, and others, eventually defined the microeconomic system (see Fig. A.1).

The development of microeconomics thus far, has roughly gone through four stages: the first stage was from the mid-17th century to the mid-19th century, which is the early or embryonic stage of microeconomics; the second stage was from the late 19th century to the early 20th century, which is the stage of neoclassical economics, when the foundation of microeconomics was laid; the third stage was from the 1930s to the 1960s, which is the establishment stage of microeconomics; the fourth stage was from the 1960s to the present day, which is the stage for further development, expansion and evolution of microeconomics.

The new developments in microeconomics in recent years are worth mentioning here:

(1) The new consumption theory, such as revealed preference, consumer choice under risks, "consumption being also household production", and others;
(2) The new theory of the firm, such as the nature of the firm, maximization models, principal-agent problem, internal organizational efficiency, non-optimizing theories, etc.;
(3) The non-equilibrium theory: Through investigating the real social economy, especially that of developing nations, this theory reveals that over a given period of time, the economies of most developing nations, even of some developed nations, are in a state of non-equilibrium, which is an important question on, supplement to, and development of the equilibrium theory.
(4) The game theory rewrote microeconomics. *Theory of Games and Economic Behavior*, co-authored by John von Neumann and Oskar Morgenstern in 1944, signified the formal establishment of the economic game theory. After half a century, by 1994, when John Forbes Nash Jr., Reinhard Selten and John Harsanyi, the three major game theorists, shared the 1994 Bank of Sweden Prize in Economic Sciences in Memory of Alfred Nobel, the game theory had been substantially enriched and developed, and reshaped the exclusive theory of microeconomics. From Antoine Augustin Cournot, Joseph Bertrand to Edward Hastings Chamberlin, economists have come to realize that market competition in reality needs, in most cases, to be explained by the oligopoly theory, and that key empirical research on oligopoly market should be conducted under the framework of "structure-behavior-performance". Developed along this line, the theory of sunk cost, the incomplete information model, the theory of individual and collective rationality, the folk theorem and other analytical techniques, have raised market analysis in modern economics to a completely new level.
(5) The public choice theory: The public choice school, represented by James M. Buchanan, Jr., Gordon Tullock and others, pioneered the application of microeconomic principles to the analysis of the demand and supply of public goods.
(6) The new institutional economics (with the property rights theory as its main content): Since the 1970s, the new institutional economics established by John Kenneth Galbraith, Karl Gunnar Myrdal, Ronald Coase, and others, has further developed microeconomic theories by incorporating such concepts as institution, rules, property rights, social behaviors and human consciousness into research. For example, theories of property rights and firms as represented by

Coase, pushed neoclassical economics forward. Subsequent to the 1980s, Douglass North pioneered the use of property rights theory to investigate the history of economics, which developed microeconomics to a new stage of institutional innovation and transformation.

(7) Information economics, which studies the individual's optimal decision under circumstances of asymmetric information, including economic analysis under imperfect information with "information cost", optimized information search and economic analysis under asymmetric information as the core: Since the 1960s, the development of information economics, for example, the view that the value of information is basically expressed via non-convexity, has overturned not only some of Marshall's established theories, but also the existence of basic equilibrium in the competition market and other related theorems. Information economics has identified the limitations of traditional microeconomic theories, and further actively promoted the development of microeconomics in the late 20th century.

It should be said that as a branch of economics, microeconomics has reached relative maturity in terms of definitions, initiation of research, research contents, methodologies, analytic tools, development trends and internal configurations.

A.2 Mezzoeconomics

Mezzoeconomics is a branch of modern economics that mainly studies regional economic units and regional economic development[1]; hence, to a certain extent, it possesses connotations of regional economics and urban economics.

The subject of research in mezzoeconomics is regional government. Regional government behavior assumes the dual attributes of "quasi-macro" (compared with a nation, its focus is on "coordination") and "quasi-micro" (pursuing maximized regional interests, possessing certain corporate characteristics). It is precisely the dual attributes or dual roles of regional governments that remedy the defects in the traditional economics system or traditional market theory, and redefine the modern economics system and modern market theory. Modern market theory states that enterprises are subjects in market competitions, and so are regional governments. The modern economics system has also demonstrated that not only are there microeconomics which studies enterprises, and macroeconomics which studies nations (or the world), but there is also mezzoeconomics which studies regional governments.

The focus of mezzoeconomics is the allocation of urban resources. Governmental administration of regional economic activities is mainly manifested in the three main functions of economic development, urban construction, and social livelihood. Corresponding to economic development are industrial resources, which are operational resources; corresponding to urban construction are urban resources, which are quasi-operational resources (with both public welfare and commercial attributes); corresponding to social livelihood are public goods and public welfare resources, which are non-operational resources. Whether urban resources should be developed as public welfare goods or operated as commercial goods depends on the financial revenues and expenditures, market demand, and affordability of the public of regional governments, and whether they are scientifically allocated also determines the competitiveness of the government in the regional market.

Mezzoeconomics thus studies regional governments' definition of the above three types of resources and their supporting policies, of which there are three key points: (1) Industrial, trade, and human resources policies correspond to operational resources (i.e., industrial resources), whose allocation principles should be "planning, guidance; support, coordination; supervision, management". Fiscal, financial, and investment policies correspond to quasi-operational resources (i.e., urban resources), whose allocation principles should be "abiding by market rules; maintaining economic order; participating in regional competition". Income, employment, and security policies correspond to non-operational resources (i.e., public welfare resources), whose allocation principles should be "general underpinning; fairness and justice; effective promotion". (2) Governments should lead foresightedly in resource allocation, that is, governments are to let enterprises do what they should do, and leave what they are unable to do or unable to do well to governments. Neither enterprises nor governments should be absent in the market. The foresighted leading by governments is to abide by market rules and rely on market to guide, coordinate and forewarn the industrial economy; to allocate, participate in and maintain the order of the urban economy; and to guarantee, underpin and promote the livelihood economy. Foresighted leading requires governments to use policies on planning, investment, consumption, pricing, taxation, interest rates, exchange rates, legislation, and others, and value, institutional, organizational, technological innovations and other measures, to effectively push forward structural reforms on the supply side or the demand side, forming a leading edge in economic growth and facilitating scientific and sustainable development of the region. (3) Value innovation plays a substantial role in driving the allocation of regional resources during the factor-driven stage; organizational innovation has multiplier effects on the allocation of regional resources during the investment-driven stage; institutional and technological innovations play decisive roles in the allocation of regional resources during the innovation-driven stage. Continuous all-round innovations in all factors throughout the process shall then promote the scientific and sustainable developments of resource allocations across all stages of regional development.

At the core of mezzoeconomics research is regional government competition, including competitions among regional governments in projects, supporting industrial chain, talents, science and technology, treasury and finance, infrastructure, import and export, environmental system, policy system, management efficiency, and others.

The basic assumptions and methods in mezzoeconomics research include: efficiency growth is the main goal of regional governments; improving total factor productivity is the main means by which regional governments compete; improving the supply-side structural reform is the basic direction for regional governments; optimizing the allocation of regional resources through planning to promote the

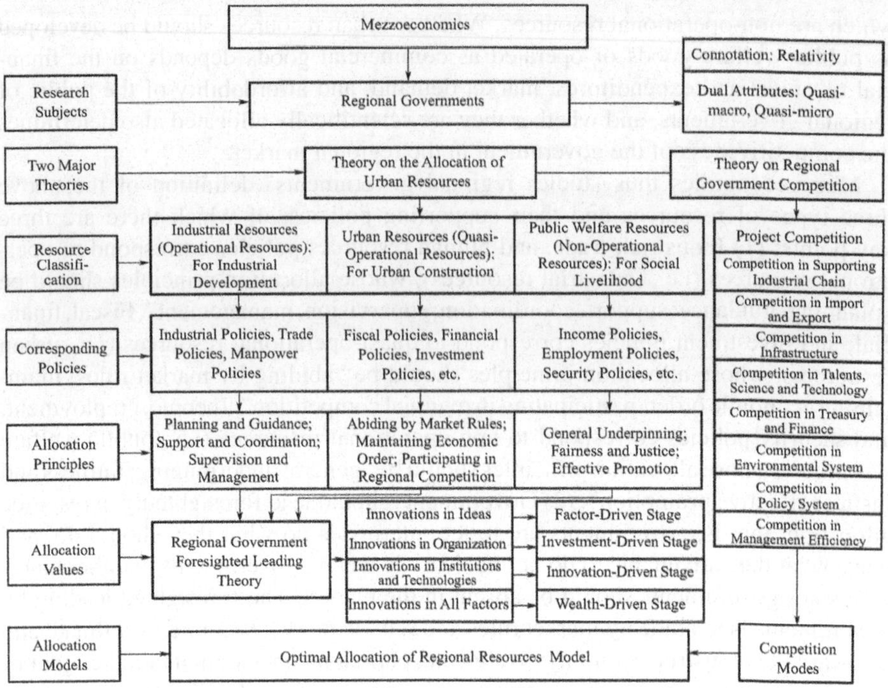

Fig. A.2 Mezzoeconomics Theory System

sustainable development of regional social economy is the competition mode for regional governments (see Fig. A.2).

Research in mezzoeconomics started rather late. In the mid-1970s, Dr. Hans-Rudolf Peters, German professor of national economics, first proposed the concept of "mezzoeconomy". In the mid-1980s, Chinese scholar Wang Shenzhi published *Mezzoeconomics* (Shanghai People's Press, 1988), which elaborated upon Peters' mezzoeconomy, and classified research subjects of mezzoeconomics into sector economy, regional economy and group economy. In 2011, I published *Foresighted Leading: Theoretical Thinking and Practice of China's Regional Economic Development*. In 2013, I co-published with Qiu Jianwei *Government Foresighted Leading: Theory and Practice of the World's Regional Economic Development*. In 2015, I co-published with Gu Wenjing *Mezzoeconomics: Innovations and Developments in Theoretical Configuration of Economics*. In 2017, I co-published with Gu Wenjing *On Regional Government Competition*. These publications have provided systematic expositions of foresighted leading by regional governments, the dual roles of regional governments, and the dual subjects in market competition, emphasizing that a mature market economy lies with the "strong effective government and strong efficient market". These theories have established the theoretical system of mezzoeconomics and clarified its prospects. The rational core in its theoretical system paves

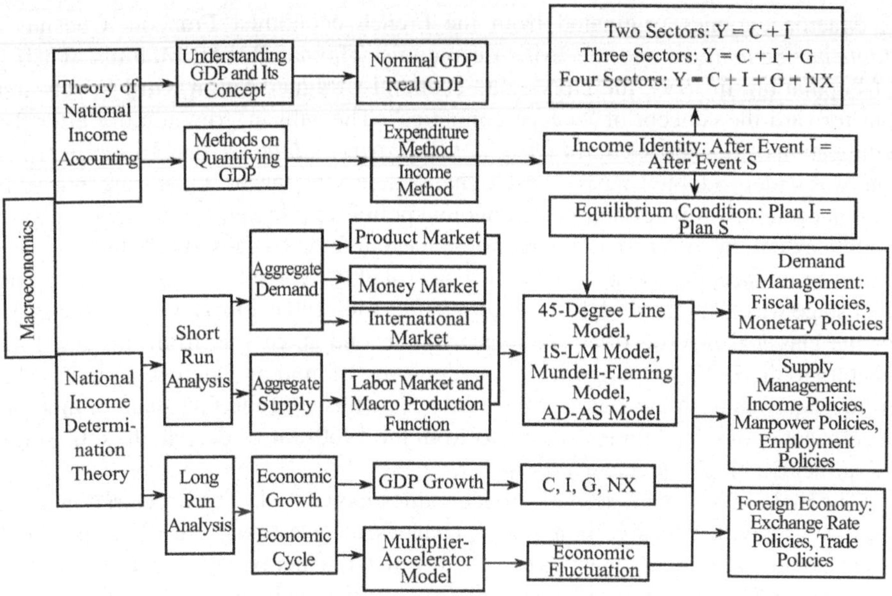

Fig. A.3 Macroeconomics Theory System

the way for economic development across the world and the construction of a new global economic governance system.

A.3 Macroeconomics

Being an independent theoretical system of economics, macroeconomics regards the activities in the overall process of national economy as its research subject. It mainly examines economic aggregates such as the employment level, national income and others, and investigates the utilization of economic resources. Modern macroeconomics includes macroeconomic theories, macroeconomic policies and macroeconometric models. Macroeconomic theories mainly include theories of national income accounting and national income determination, which encompass theories on employment, inflation, economic cycles, economic growth and others.

Macroeconomics mainly studies economic growth, economic cycle, unemployment, inflation, national finance, international trade, etc. Research indicators are mainly national income, ratio of aggregate social consumption, savings and investment to national income, the amount and speed of currency circulation, price level, interest rates, population size and its growth rate, employment and unemployment rates, national budget and deficit, import and export trade, and balance of payment, etc (see Fig. A.3).

Macroeconomics originated from the French economist François Quesnay's *Tableau Économique* and the British economist Thomas Robert Malthus' Theory of Population. In 1933, the Norwegian economist Ragnar Anton Kittil Frisch first put forward the concept of "macroeconomics". The subject grew rapidly after the publication of Keynes' *General Theory of Employment, Interest, and Money* in 1936, and was widely adopted across Western nations, serving the policy of state intervention in economy. Keynesian macroeconomic policies promoted economic growth to a great extent; however, state intervention in economy also caused problems.

Since its inception, macroeconomics has roughly evolved over four stages: The first stage was from the mid-17th century to the mid-19th century, which is the early or the classical macroeconomics stage. The second stage was from the late 19th century to the 1930s, which is the foundation stage of modern macroeconomics. The third stage was from the 1930s to the 1960s, which is the founding stage of modern macroeconomics. The fourth stage was from the 1960s onwards, which is the stage of further development and evolution.

The main views of modern macroeconomics include: (1) The acceleration principle suggests that to a certain extent, changes in investment are the causes and effects of changes in national income, from which the theory of interaction between "accelerator" and "multiplier" is derived. (2) The price problem discussed in macroeconomics is the general price level. In the national income determination theory, the general price level depends mainly on the aggregate demand level, whilst changes in the aggregate demand level affect and are greatly affected by monetary supply and demand. Changes in monetary supply and total price level are closely related, hence monetary analysis plays an important role in macroeconomics. (3) It is believed in macroeconomics that governments should and in fact could adjust the aggregate demand through fiscal policies, monetary policies, and other measures so as to ease the periodical economic fluctuations and attain full employment without inflation.

There are still numerous defects in macroeconomics currently, which include mainly:

(1) Macroeconomics as it is currently, has not completely grasped the modern market system. Horizontally, the modern market system should include three levels of market—global, national, and state or provincial; vertically, it should include six subsystems: market factor system, market organization system, market legal system, market supervision system, market environment system, and market infrastructure. The modern market economy is a large and complete market system, and any theory attempting to explain this system without considering market segmentation is deemed to be short on vision and lacking in clarity on thoughts.

(2) Macroeconomics as it is currently, has a relatively narrow concept of "macro", which should include two levels: for provinces and cities, the nation is the macro level; for nations, the globe is the macro level. Wherein today, when the modern economic system has spread all over the "global village", to discuss a nation's macroeconomy regardless of its relations to and the impacts of the global economic system would clearly have too many defects.

(3) Macroeconomics as it is currently, needs a deeper understanding of the government and market combination modes. A mature market economy should be an economy of "strong effective government plus strong efficient market". Effective government can be classified into three types: weak, semi-strong and strong; efficient market can also be classified into three types: weak, semi-strong and strong. The combination of effective governments and efficient markets can theoretically generate at least nine modes, but only "strong effective government plus strong efficient market" is the best mode for government and market combination. It is the goal for nations across the world in theory and practice, and should be explored profoundly in macroeconomics.

As such, it is increasingly urgent to reform and innovate macroeconomics. I think we can start with the following:

(1) Establishing the notion of a modern market system: Microeconomics mainly studies enterprises and focuses on the allocation of industrial resources, these being the first level of market economic activities. Mezzoeconomics mainly studies regional governments and focuses on the allocation of urban resources, these being the second level of market economic activities. Macroeconomics mainly studies (established) individual national subjects and (established and to-be-established intergovernmental) international economic institutions and focuses on the allocation, coordination and standardization of industrial, urban and public welfare resources, these being the third level of market economic activities. Macroeconomics should be based on the first and second levels of market economic activities, so as to formulate and improve the rules for market economic activities at the third level, which is the highest level.

    Furthermore, at the national level, macroeconomics should focus on national income accounting and distribution theory, which includes a nation's macroeconomic fiscal policies, monetary policies, exchange rate policies and supervision policies. The national income generation and determination theory, and its corresponding policies on industries, trade, human resources, income, employment, social security, and others, should be placed into mezzoeconomics research.

(2) Establishing the path towards a mature market economy: A mature market economy combines strong effective government with strong efficient market. Regional governments have dual codes of conduct: pursing the maximized regional interests on the one hand, which requires them to participate in market competition, and coordinating super-regional interests on the other hand. Regional governments must also abide by market rules and maintain market order whilst competing with each other in the market economic system. On the national front, macroeconomics must face and solve such problems as coordinating and standardizing regional government competition, establishing and improving legal and supervision systems and social credit system, in order to encourage them to compete fully in the market economy system, and achieve fairness, justice and win-win cooperation.

(3) Strengthening the importance of macroeconomic coordination in the international economy: Macroeconomics should focus on the macroeconomies at the

international level, such as restructuring international economic governance institutions, innovating tools for international economic development, improving international economic regulatory standards and norms, and building up new engines at the global level for investment, innovation and regulation. This is where the significance of contemporary macroeconomics lies.

(4) Forging a new international economic order: That is, formulating corresponding international economic norms on competitions for the allocation of industrial resources across the world, based on the principles of fairness and efficiency; formulating corresponding intergovernmental governance rules on competitions for the allocation of urban resources across the world, based on the principles of win-win cooperation; formulating corresponding rules on international security order for the supply system of global public goods, based on the principles of peace and stability. In any case, to establish the global economic governance system of the "Four I's"—Innovation, Invigoration, Interconnection and Inclusiveness—in the global economy, a sound matching macroeconomics system is needed.

Note

The concept of "region" is of course a relative one: globally a nation is a region, while nationally a province or a city is a region. Therefore, to examine a nation's competition in global economy from a mezzoeconomics perspective would also deepen the economic research under new circumstances.

Epilogue

The book, *New Economic Engine: Effective Government and Efficient Market*, was finished in about three months, but my thoughts and explorations had lasted for more than ten years. It can be said that it is not only the result of my years of hard work, but also the fruit of our common wisdom.

In 2005, I served as Secretary of the Shunde District Committee of the CPC in Foshan City, Guangdong Province, which ranked first among more than 2,800 county economies in the country. Based on my experience accumulated whilst pursuing a Ph.D. in economics at Peking University, I took time off my busy schedule to explore the ideologies behind the mainstream schools of economics led by Adam Smith, John Maynard Keynes, and others, and proposed the idea of "Government Foresighted Leading (GFL)". In 2011, I published the monograph *Foresighted Leading* (later published in English by Springer, Germany). In 2013, I co-authored with Qiu Jianwei and published *Government Foresighted Leading: Theory and Practice of the World's Regional Economic Development* (later published in English by Routledge, UK). In 2015, I co-authored with Gu Wenjing to publish the monograph *Mezzoeconomics: Innovations and Developments in Theoretical Configuration of Economics* (later published in English by American Academic Press). And in 2017, I co-authored with Gu Wenjing again to publish the monograph *On Regional Government Competition* (later published in English by Routledge).

On the completion of this book, I would like to thank Qiu Jianwei and Gu Wenjing for our original cooperation, which has provided a solid foundation for this work. I would also like to thank the translator, Ethan Chung, for his efforts in translating this book, and thank Wu Hao from Beijing Foreign Studies University, and Yi Lu, Zhao Yaru and Shi Linan from Foreign Language Teaching and Research Press for their hard work in editing and publishing this book, whose meticulousness, rigorousness, willingness to discuss, and persistence have left an indelible impression on me. Special gratitude goes to my wife, Zhang Biying, for without her silent yet enduring companionship, encouragement, dedication and support, I could not have completed this research with my heavy work schedule.

Y. Chen, *New Economic Engine: Effective Government and Efficient Market*, China Academic Library, https://doi.org/10.1007/978-981-15-2922-1

Many thanks to this great nation! Many thanks to this great era! This book is dedicated to the 40th anniversary of China's Reform and Opening Up.

Chen Yunxian
Guangzhou
May 19, 2018

The manufacturer's authorised representative in the EU is Springer Nature Customer Service Centre GmbH, Europaplatz 3, 69115 Heidelberg, Germany. If you have any concerns regarding our products, please contact ProductSafety@springernature.com

Printed and bound by CPI Group (UK) Ltd, Croydon, CR0 4YY
30/09/2026
02225261-0010